Stress in turbulent times

Stress in turbulent times

Ashley Weinberg
Senior Lecturer in Psychology, Directorate of Psychology,
University of Salford, UK

and

Cary Cooper
Pro Vice Chancellor (External Relations) and
Professor of Organizational Psychology and Health, Lancaster
University, UK

First published 2012 by
PALGRAVE MACMILLAN

Palgrave Macmillan in the UK is an imprint of Macmillan Publishers Limited,
registered in England, company number 785998, of Houndmills, Basingstoke,
Hampshire RG21 6XS.

Palgrave Macmillan in the US is a division of St Martin's Press LLC,
175 Fifth Avenue, New York, NY 10010.

Palgrave Macmillan is the global academic imprint of the above companies
and has companies and representatives throughout the world.

Palgrave® and Macmillan® are registered trademarks in the United States,
the United Kingdom, Europe and other countries.

ISBN: 978–0–230–23560–1

This book is printed on paper suitable for recycling and made from fully
managed and sustained forest sources. Logging, pulping and manufacturing
processes are expected to conform to the environmental regulations of the
country of origin.

A catalogue record for this book is available from the British Library.

A catalog record for this book is available from the Library of Congress.

10 9 8 7 6 5 4 3 2 1
21 20 19 18 17 16 15 14 13 12

Printed and bound in Great Britain by
CPI Antony Rowe, Chippenham and Eastbourne

I would like to dedicate this book to my wonderful wife Anne, my fantastic children James and Lottie, and my supportive Mum and Dad – thank you all for all your love and encouragement. To those good people who have kindly contributed to the case studies in this book, I would like to thank you for sharing your experiences so willingly. I would also like to acknowledge the encouragement of my co-author and those at Palgrave Macmillan including Stephen Rutt, Eleanor Davey Corrigan, Hannah Fox, Vidhya Jayaprakash and the production team in Chennai, who provided encouragement and worked so hard to bring this book to the shelves.

Contents

CHAPTER 1

The fall of capitalism?

'I am living in a country which has seen its financial system reach meltdown; there have been mass protests on the streets by an angry public facing an uncertain future; there is widespread disenchantment with politicians and parts of the media and law enforcement; and regular allegations of corruption, cover-up or greed are leveled at organizations which should have known better. Where am I?'

The answer is, this could be one of many countries at many points in time, but it is likely to be yours right now! In some way or other, the events and crises mentioned affect everyone. Whether it is because of job loss or the threat of it, money worries or the impact on our families and communities, we are acutely aware of the importance to us of these turbulent times and of the emotions that accompany them. There is a sense of loss and no little drop in faith in the systems which have underpinned modern, economically developed societies. So, who do we turn to for answers? The appeal of fictional characters like Harry Potter is understandable, but what we are apt to take for granted, or even forget, is our own set of capabilities. The superhuman may not be necessary were we able to recognize the inbuilt human potential to adapt and survive, which has served us well for many thousands of years. If we already possess the necessary qualities to cope with turbulent times, then what is the nature of the challenges we face and how well are we equipped to deal with them? This book sets out to explore the answers.

The nature of turbulent times

There is one kind of stress, but there are many types of pressure. All humans share the same set of responses to challenge – whether physical or psychological – and, although we may experience the outcomes slightly differently, we are facing the dilemma of whether to fight, flee or freeze. We can of course benefit from the impetus that the right amount of pressure can give us, but over a period of time and at levels in excess of our abilities to cope, the consequences can be most detrimental. An economic crisis may seem too abstract to cause us to choose between fight and flight, but there can be little doubt that its fallout produces exactly the types of pressures from which we would be happy to be released by one means or another. Threats to jobs, incomes, homes and education, and uncertainties over our ability to meet daily needs have been unleashed on a scale not seen since the Great Depression of the 1930s following the collapse of the stock market in the Wall Street crash of 29 October 1929. Those who remember that economic catastrophe also recall what followed in terms of political and social upheaval on a global scale. It remains to be seen whether parallel events will register their own impact, but it is likely that the year 2008 will be long associated with the near meltdown of the global economic system. Reports of the death of capitalism may, to paraphrase Mark Twain, have been much exaggerated, but there was no denying the economic disaster and its consequences.

This chapter sets the scene to the challenges we face by examining the salient economic events which have had such far-reaching effects on nations, organizations and the individuals who comprise them. In the rest of the book we will explore the psychological consequences in different aspects of our lives in order to understand how and why we might respond to such globally felt threats and dilemmas.

Are we living in turbulent times? Is the beginning of the twenty-first century more challenging for our species than any other time? Perhaps there is a 'yes', 'no' or 'maybe' on your lips? Certainly, whenever there is change or the prospect of change, there is turbulence in our lives as we try to come to terms with a new reality and prepare to adjust. As a species we are fairly attuned to change – social upheaval in our own lifetimes has taught us this much. 'Change is constant' is one ironic truism, but are our times more difficult than over fifty years ago when, in the aftermath of World War II, the Cold War was at a peak and the threat of nuclear annihilation a real prospect? Then, the conflict between ideologies was reflected in so much of political and economic life, yet at the same time there was a new dawn in popular culture in music, literature and the arts. Compare that to over a hundred years ago when the age of empires was nearing its end with the 'war to end all wars' and one of the deadliest flu pandemics ever. Is it fairer to say that for many the sources of turbulence could not have been considered greater, or that every era features its own demons? Even 150 years ago, the families of both authors were clinging to daily existence, made treacherous by regimes which tolerated the prejudice-fuelled excesses of the pogroms in Eastern Europe and by unsafe and low-paid employment in the industrialized West. Unfortunately, such themes persist to varying degrees, and within recent memory atrocities in Rwanda and in the former Yugoslavia show that the Nazi Holocaust was not an isolated evil. Yet the ability of peoples to emerge from such dark days with purpose and success, even after the migrations of millions, is clear. For example, the largest movement of people in a single wave, from Eastern Europe in the late 1800s, contributed to the success of many nations, including the United States. Indeed the history of civilizations, whether ancient Rome or modern-day United Kingdom, shows the positive impact of immigration on future prosperity. The key to this has been the will of peoples to survive and learn from each other to ensure a more secure future, one that is safer from the haunting threats of the past.

Compared to then, life expectancy in many countries has risen as medical and technological advances have fostered increased health awareness, while global aid is more effectively coordinated. As a species we can point to so many achievements in international cooperation and, in many areas, to positive social change once considered unthinkable. Yet the threat of environmental disaster, as well as from politically and financially motivated crime and terrorism continue to plague many nations. Against the uneven background of human progress, the challenges facing us naturally make these turbulent times, as the themes of history are also the themes of today: wars between nations and wars which transcend physical borders; conflicts within countries caused by tyranny and corruption; crippling national debt; environmental disasters; disease and famine continue to abound (see Table 1.1). A handful of news headlines from recent years confirms the huge scale of the challenges to humanity worldwide as tens of thousands of people are reported to have been killed in the wars in Iraq and Afghanistan, thousands have been drowned or displaced by floods in the low-lying areas of Japan, Bangladesh and Australia and thousands are reported dead each year in drug wars and trafficking on the US–Mexico border. As individuals it is hard to contemplate

Table 1.1   Examples of crises and events in the period January 2010–August 2011

Country	Nature of disaster/crisis
New Zealand	Earthquake strikes capital Christchurch
Japan	Tsunami destroys coastal towns and nuclear facilities threaten to melt down
Haiti	Earthquake
Pakistan	Floods and terrorist attacks
Greece	Mass protests against austerity measures
Iran	Mass protests against the government
Tunisia and Egypt	'Arab Spring' – overthrow of long-established regimes by public demand
Libya	Civil war
Syria	Crackdown on popular uprisings
Myanmar	Mass protests against the regime leading to release of the opposition's leader
Afghanistan	Terrorist attacks; continuing occupation by Nato forces
USA	Storms wreak havoc across Midwestern states and eastern seaboard
Somalia	Worst famine for many decades; civil war and piracy
Norway	Terrorist atrocities

the scale of such suffering, or indeed what part we can play in alleviating it, but stories such as the success in rescuing thirty-three Chilean miners buried underground after a mining accident or of finding survivors in the rubble of an earthquake are more easily digestible. Similarly there is widespread admiration for the endeavors of peoples to stand up for their rights in Myanmar and in the 'Arab Spring', which show the potential victories of human strengths when working together with common goals.

Whether it is a global financial crisis which undermines our lives, or other forms of disaster, what is clear is that our species desires to persevere, regroup and reemerge. This book is about the nature, strength and frailty of that human spirit and how, in times of great challenge, such as economic catastrophe, that spirit strives to carve a brighter future.

Worlds colliding

The images of economic turbulence have different meanings depending on our perspectives. For some it is the picture of a stock market trader slumped on the floor looking exhausted and defeated at the end of a disastrous day's trading; for others it is the face of a worker looking on with tears in her eyes at the announcement of the closure of her workplace. Beyond that, one can imagine the repercussions in people's homes up and down the country as they begin to question how they will afford the lifestyle they had previously expected to pursue – including the price of the roof over their heads.

In 2008 and not for the last time, capitalism appeared to collapse. This was the worst economic crisis in Westernized countries since the Great Depression. By contrast, in 1990 communist regimes in Eastern Europe crumbled and people were seen to rejoice by breaking off bits of the Berlin Wall for souvenirs – symbols of freedom. The difference between the denouement of communism and the near-toppling of capitalism can be summed up by comparing the meaning of the bricks and masonry which represented the literal destruction of each system. For those in the formerly communist Eastern European states, the pulling down of the wall in East Berlin – built to keep in and repress a population – was symbolic of breaking free. More recently, for those living in economies reliant on a market-based system which encouraged materialism and home ownership, the bricks of their own homes now represented prisons of debt, poised to deprive them of their financial independence for years to come. The impact could be felt in countries as far apart as Japan, which had its worst economic performance for fifty years in the first quarter of 2009, and in the United Kingdom, where a government-sponsored program to build schools was slashed as the value of land collapsed and loans dried up.

To understand the psychological impact of economic disaster it is important to try to understand both the human behavior which led to it as well as the emotional and practical consequences for so many. In examining these in more detail we can pinpoint both positive and negative human traits which lead us into crises and also show us the way out. Where these two sides of the human equation met was exemplified by the 'Classic case of two worlds colliding' (Clark, 2010a), when the head office of the Bear Stearns Bank, on Madison Avenue, New York, was invaded by hundreds of protesters angry that the loans system which had enabled them to buy their homes had collapsed as a result of what many perceived as the malpractice of overpaid financial employees. The demonstrators accused the bankers of greed, while the financiers pointed to the need for their services, which they claimed had created wealth and fuelled aspirations for the rest of the nation. To some extent this pattern has continued in the public consciousness ever since, with each side justifying its own position. Such collisions of viewpoints have even led to death in an Athens bank destroyed by fire during the protests against cuts in public spending as well as to death threats against the prominent former bank executive Fred Goodwin in the United Kingdom.

Underpinning the solution to the economic mess are considerable ironies – that the people who do not have access to considerable wealth via large financial bonuses have contributed money via taxes to support the continued operation of banks under threat of collapse and that, in the aftermath, thousands of traders who work for these banks have continued to claim rewards well in excess of the annual pay of the average taxpayer. In 2009, when many banks showed deficits, 'financiers took home an average performance-linked pay cheque of $99,200' (Clark, 2010a). How did it come to this? Should it be inevitable that people within the same society could be so distanced from one another? Did failure to consider the social and economic consequences of unwise investments cause the problems in the first place and was this simply the transference of the cost of human frailty from one section of society to another? Whatever the motivation, attempts to curb the bonuses paid in the banking sector seemed to bear limited fruit. The European Union announced restrictions on the nature and scale of bankers' rewards, including the deferral of 40 percent of bonuses for between three to five years in order to take future performance into account. However, there remained no limit on bankers' pay, and up to 20 percent of the largest bonuses could be taken in the form of cash (BBC News, 2010). Not surprisingly, the success of the ethos of restraint received mixed reviews, although the UK Exchequer claimed it saw positive signs in the drop in value of total banking bonuses from £19 billion in 2007 to £14 billion in 2010–11 (*The Guardian*, 2011a). In the United States, Treasury Secretary Timothy Geithner and President Obama were vocal in their criticism of bankers' bonuses, yet despite limited success in getting some of these repaid by failing institutions – such as insurers and financial services organization American International Group (AIG) – and emergency congressional legislation to impose a 90 percent tax on cash bonuses, it was acknowledged that more fundamental change was awaited.

Case study 1.1   A brief exchange on the exchange floor

'How's it going?' asked the young man, keen to learn more about the currency exchange system from his senior colleague, who replies, 'Fine thanks, have a seat. ... Oh, just let me take this call; they've been trying to get hold of me.' He pauses. 'Nine million you say? Okay, will do.' The young man listens intently. After the call ends, the experienced partner continues: 'People are dumping dollars at the moment and buying up other currencies to make money on the exchange rates.' He says, 'This whole delay in the Americans deciding on their debt ceiling is the reason.' 'Yeah, can you believe they're within a week of the whole thing crashing down?' replies the young man. Meanwhile, the exchange dealer glances at his computer screen and presses a couple of keys, replying, 'They'll never let it come to that – it's all politics really. ... [S]orry, I just had to send that off, my client wanted to buy $9 million.' His junior colleague smiles, more in amazement than anything else – he had just witnessed more money than he could imagine transferred in the blink of an eye.

Death in the marketplace

So there it was. People switched on their televisions to hear the words they had never expected: the good times were over, and economic security was a thing of the past. The gloss of established prosperity had been wiped away almost overnight. *USA Today* proclaimed: 'If the US economy were a car, all of its warning lights must be flashing red' (19 March

2008). The shock turned to reality as many found they could not access their bank accounts or learned that the share price on which their savings and pensions depended was spiraling downward and almost out of existence. The unthinkable had happened – banks began to crash. After the British government had taken control of a major bank, Northern Rock in 2007, the following spring Bear Stearns was the first to require rescue in the United States. However, these were but a prelude to the autumn of 2008, which saw Wall Street investment bank Lehman Brothers fall in full view of transatlantic government observers, closely followed by UK high street bank Halifax Bank of Scotland (HBOS) being taken over by Lloyds Banking Group. According to former US treasury secretary Henry Paulson, the fall of insurer AIG – whose policies protected a string of leading banks and securities firms, including Goldman Sachs, Citigroup and JP Morgan – would have signaled a 'complete collapse' of the global financial system (Clark, 2010a). If, on the evening of 16 September 2008, the US government had not provided the $85 billion to prop up AIG the end of trust in the capitalist system may well have followed, and with it the basis for financial trading(Clark, 2010a). In a similar vein, the UK government, led by Prime Minister Gordon Brown, ploughed £37 billion into propping up the Royal Bank of Scotland and HBOS/Lloyds and, in conjunction with the Bank of England, began a process of 'quantitative easing'. This allowed more money to be injected into the financial system as a method of diluting the impact of the shortage of lending, which had naturally resulted from the paralysis affecting the ailing banks.

The accepted history is that the seeds of this economic crisis began in the American sub-prime mortgage lending market, with the overzealous issuing of loans to millions of would-be property owners normally considered high-risk in terms of their ability to repay. Even without a comprehensive understanding of the economics of supply and demand, it is easy to see why pouring money into what might be considered a bottomless pit could only lead to one outcome: 'misery', as no doubt Charles Dickens' Mr Micawber would have observed. Attempts to patch up the growing problems via the use of insurance against huge losses, or even reckless 'short-selling' to undermine confidence in other companies, demonstrated how careful consideration for the management of risk had either no impact or was not done. Once the pillars supporting the money markets began to crumble, governments had little option but to intervene with taxpayers' money on an almost unimaginable scale to prevent meltdown of the international financial system.

During the following months, people arrived at work to find emergency meetings in which jobs to be scrapped were listed on big screens, while others turned up at work to find factory gates or shop doors permanently locked. Others did not get this far, already hearing on the news that their organization had gone bust, including employees of UK high street stalwart, Woolworths. US automobile manufacturing giants General Motors and Chrysler filed for bankruptcy and having wiped their debts clear progressed to profit, while firms which relied on centuries of consumer appeal, such as 250-year old Irish-based manufacturers of fine china and glassware, Waterford Wedgewood, were rescued by overseas investors. Many other companies for which so many had worked so hard had gone. Eighteen months after September 2008, unemployment rose to 9.6 percent in the US and 7.8 percent in the UK. Some countries, such as Denmark and Austria, experienced smaller increases in the numbers of jobless owing to what the European Union social affairs commissioner, Vladimir Spidla, acknowledged was a more effective combination of social protection – such as social security systems to soften the impact of unemployment – and flexibility for business organizations (Clark, 2009).

Governments of various political hues tried to put into action their own economic recovery plans. In the United States, the election of Barack Obama as president came as a beacon of hope to many only a few months after these cataclysmic economic events, but the decision to pump a further $780 billion into the banking system in 2009 created discord within the nation's political parties and took to $1.7 trillion the total in financial measures attempting to put the brakes on the crisis. This was despite considerable opposition from Republicans and Democrats in the US Congress. Without this action, White House economic experts claim, a further 8.5 million jobs would have been lost and economic output would have dropped by an additional 6.5 percent (Clark, 2010b). This did not stop similar political brinkmanship taking place in the summer of 2011, placing the United States within one week of becoming financially insolvent. Meanwhile, the change of UK governments in the spring of 2010 ended the Keynesian-inspired strategies which had delayed cuts in public spending in order to keep money flowing in the economy and 'recapitalize' the system. Instead, the Conservative-Liberal Democrat coalition pressed ahead with spending cuts and tax rises to lessen the massive national debt. For critics of this approach, the threat of a 'double-dip' recession seemed more likely. This would mean that after the initial economic storm, signs of recovery would fade as financial cuts slashed public sector jobs and fed into a cycle of stagnating, rather than increasing, economic activity. In other words, overzealous cutbacks would reduce the numbers of people in work and therefore the amount of money spent by consumers, thus contributing to a second recession. Forecasts of economic success or failure abounded, as after the initial bank crashes and the severe impact on the private sector, including the housing and motor industries, the United Kingdom faced an unprecedented fall in public sector services. This would result from job cuts of between 330,000 and 490,000, according to the government fiscal watchdog, the Office for Budget Responsibility (*The Guardian*, 2010a). Before these employment reductions actually kicked in, almost a million UK private sector jobs had disappeared in the two years either side of March 2010. In addition to the social and economic cost, UK organizations paid out £13.4 billion over three years in redundancy payments to reduce their staff numbers, averaging £9,362 per employee in 2010–11 (*The Guardian*, 2011c). However, this was still lower than the total figure of £14 billion for bankers' bonuses in 2010–11 (BBC News, 2011).

Just one facet of projected cuts was the reduction in funding of the UK's National Health Service by up to 25 percent and of the police force by 20 percent, with their likely impacts on patient care, public order and jobs. Obliteration of UK government funding for university courses in many fields threatened academic departments with closure, and the decision to raise the cap on university tuition fees from £3,000 to £9,000 per year of study led to riotous scenes around Parliament in December 2010. The UK coalition government anticipated that new growth in the private sector would create more jobs than those lost, but by 2011 there were approximately 2.5 million unemployed, compared to 1.6 million in 2008. The barometers of social discontent, which at the hard end include public protest and disorder and at the softer end of the spectrum comprise songs of satire, already suggested that 'there may be trouble ahead'. It might be predicted that rising crime statistics reflect discontent, and also the motivation to find unlawful means of income; notwithstanding the differences in measurement methods, there are indications on both sides of the Atlantic that this may be true. The most startling of these was provided in 2011 by the summer riots in many of England's major conurbations which appeared to catch the authorities unprepared and at times helpless to defend city centers. Even within the United Kingdom, different statistics emerge from the police and the British Crime Survey, with the latter showing that domestic burglary had increased by 14 percent between 2009 and 2011 (Home Office/ONS, 2011). Personal and household crimes in the United Kingdom – including the theft of unattended property from gardens and businesses, as well as personal items left unguarded, such as wallets – also increased by 10 percent prior to the riots. Meanwhile, violence against individuals fell during the period 2006–07 to 2010–11 by 11–21 percent. A similar pattern emerged in the United States, with the estimated rate of burglaries increasing by 2 percent over the five-year period

2005–09, and violent crime against individuals decreasing by 5.2 percent during this time (FBI, 2009). Notwithstanding the vagaries of such data, it could be concluded that in times of recession, material possessions are increasingly targeted, but there is less inclination overall to commit violence against our fellow citizens. One might even suggest that within some areas of criminal activity, there is a greater recognition that in personal terms everyone has enough to contend with.

The one feature of this recession which differs from those of the past is the extent of international cooperation to combat the economic crisis. For example, the synchronization of decreases in bank interest rates across the globe and the use of government bailouts to save the financial industry were on a scale never seen before. The reasons for this included structural developments, such as the advent of the World Economic Forum, which has met annually at Davos-Klosters in Switzerland since 1971, and the regular summits by the members of the G8 and G20 countries designed to promote international agreement on a range of objectives. These feature economically and socially engaged nations discussing action to combat a number of challenges, including climate change as well as financial developments. Such levels of cooperation were notably absent during the Great Depression. At the 'Preliminary Conference with a view to concerted economic action' held in 1930, only eleven countries put their names to an agreement not to raise tariffs, and this subsequently declined to seven! At the time, the ensuing tariff steps, such as those imposed by the United States, proved disastrous for ailing exports worldwide. An additional motivator for current levels of cooperation is the political fear factor, as every government knows the price it is likely to pay if the economy suffers irreparable damage on its own watch. Having carefully crafted a reputation as a 'safe pair of hands' in guiding the economy, UK Prime Minister Gordon Brown felt the best policy at the 2010 general election was to admit responsibility and ask the country for latitude. In saving his party from electoral disaster, Brown was successful to a point, but not enough to stop his party's defeat or the end of his own leadership role.

National reputations were also at risk among the fast-shifting sands of economic instability. German Chancellor Angela Merkel signaled the likely dire effects on investors' faith in Europe if Greece was allowed to default on its €8.5 billion loan from its continental partners, which had been designed to help it deal with spiraling national debt. As a sign of the international cooperation outlined above, leaders from sixteen Eurozone countries met in May 2010 to agree a financial aid package. Shockwaves similar to those after the collapse of the US bank, Lehman Brothers, shuddered across the EU on both occasions. Meanwhile, thousands of newly built dwellings which stood empty across Irish cities were a portent that the process of international financial rescue process was to be repeated later in the year. The government of Ireland finally accepted that its own dire situation was beyond retrieval, and sought an economic bailout from the EU and International Monetary Fund as another prime minister, in this case Brian Cowen, 'walked the plank' to political oblivion. The credit ratings by agencies, such as Standard & Poor's, added resonance to these nation-sized crises, warning that similar catastrophes were facing the Iberian Peninsula if action was not quickly taken. In the spring of 2011, Portugal followed the precedents set by Greece and Ireland in asking for international financial help, while Spain and Italy braced themselves for their own challenges. The process did not stop there either, as in July Eurozone countries met again to agree a second bailout plan for Greece, in the wake of massive public protests against austerity measures and a temporary siege of parliament in Athens. This occurred at a time of financial 'stress tests' which indicated the precarious footing of increasing numbers of financial institutions and, potentially, the European currency itself. The downgrading of Italy's debt rating in the autumn of 2011 threatened to increase its cost of borrowing and made it the next country to suffer from a contagion of fear over the Eurozone debt crisis.

The human cost in emotions

Table 1.2   The balance of emotions in turbulent times

Positive emotions	Negative emotions
Determination	Greed
Bounce-backability	Blame
Perspective	Anger
Resilience	Disgust

The greed of bankers has been seen by many as the cause of the whole problem, and yet the sense of injustice felt by ordinary taxpayers has translated into anger against governments that the salvaged the banks. The publicized conviction of Ponzi scheme operators like Bernard L. Madoff in the United States brought little comfort (or reimbursement) to the defrauded, who lost an estimated $18 billion. There remained disgust about the persisting bonus culture for those in the financial sector who demanded a right to be richly rewarded. This pervading emotion appeared to outweigh the 'bounce-backability' of less powerful individuals who fought to keep their jobs, by for example reopening their local Woolworths store. Meanwhile, the people of Iceland also showed, via public referenda, their determination not to pay for the havoc created by their own country's banks.

The human cost of the crisis

For those immediately affected by the crisis, the initial shock and feeling of numbness gave way to another more unpleasant emotion. Panic began to set in, which grew like a fire. How will I pay the rent or the mortgage? Will the children have to change schools if we move? Can we afford to keep the car? How much money have we to buy food? And so a monetary crisis begins to hit countless households. Like a previously dormant volcano the economy erupts, and hundreds of thousands of people, who had made their living on the seemingly tranquil slopes of relative security and prosperity, risk being swept away in an unforgiving river of debt, misery and financial hardship.

People respond differently to such widespread emotions of panic and anxiety. Some take stock and make decisions about their futures before setting off on their chosen path to recovery. Along the way they are joined by like-minded others who have reached similar conclusions and with whom they will have to compete for the safer economic ground. Many struggle to come to terms with the accompanying emotions – whether their own or those of others close to them – and feel the downward pull of negative strain which renders them less capable of rational or positive thought. Some are able to confront their feelings and find comfort and support in sharing their experiences. Meanwhile, many who are used to being in control of their lives cannot begin to consider the consequences of giving up that control.

We all carry enduring images of events, particularly when emotional suffering is involved. At the height of the financial crisis in 2008, I was taking my usual motorway route to work over the Barton Bridge several hundred feet above the Manchester–Liverpool Ship Canal. A smart-looking saloon car was parked on the hard shoulder, and in the air to the side of the bridge hovered a police helicopter. Emergency personnel in fluorescent jackets were looking over the railings at something below. The abandoned vehicle and the edgy presence of helpless rescuers told their own story. The tumultuous storm of economic catastrophe appeared to have claimed another victim. Similar tales had emerged from eyewitness accounts of desperate acts among the New York skyscrapers during the 1929 Wall Street crash. The onset of panic and helplessness is obviously not the sole domain of economic meltdown, but is a reflection of personal loss which renders the individual hopeless. This is mirrored at both ends of the spectrum of economic endeavor and disillusionment. The suicide rate in China among rural-dwelling women, left behind by husbands moving to the cities to take up work, is globally among the highest. Just as sad is the rising frequency of self-inflicted deaths among 20–35 year olds in Chinese cities, claiming a quarter of a million fatalities annually (*The Guardian*, 2005). In Japan the pressure of work and a cultural disposition for job-related pressures to dominate employees' lives has led to a word in the language for 'suicide from overwork': 'karojisatsu'.

Case study 1.2   The emotional cost of job uncertainty

Michelle is a college graduate who, after her career in sales had ended, has been looking for almost two years for stable, full-time employment. Her current part-time job in a workplace undergoing cuts means she can use the skills acquired during her degree, but she and her colleagues are faced with staving off the threat of unemployment and, in the meantime, feeling unable to benefit from the positive aspects of their job. Without full-time work, Michelle struggles with meeting her mortgage payments, but also she has noticed a change in her demeanor.

'I know I shouldn't be blaming myself,' Michelle says. 'I keep saying to myself: it's not me, it's the system which is wrong.' Clearly intelligent, she appears by turns confident and then tearful, made vulnerable by the rigors of working as hard as possible to fight off financial troubles and also to impress her new employers sufficiently to gain a stronger foothold. 'I guess my self-belief has taken a beating – I feel that I don't have much control over what's going on.'

The edgy-sounding voice on the other end of the phone belonged to an ex-student of mine, who had worked in the banking sector and now found herself jobless and thousands of miles from home. This same week that barely controlled edginess resonated in a plain request for some coins from a homeless juggler on the streets near a university – the gulf in material possessions and expectations could not have been greater, but the waste of talent was unmistakable and scarily similar. Their demeanors shared the same hint of desperation – willing to work in any way possible to earn enough to get by – and seeking hope from a friendly face or voice. From among those fortunate enough to have a job, albeit in an uncertain UK public sector, an education marketing officer reflected on the demand for mental health training from overseas clients, but eventually admitted the dire need for this training among staff in her own institution. A traffic warden welcomed the opportunity to shelter from the rain and told how his employer, the city council, were re-introducing evening parking charges, having kept their pledge to abolish them only a few years before, as they could no longer afford to miss out on millions in potential revenue. That same day, the Manchester City Council led the UK national news headlines by announcing that a projected redundancy scheme involving 1,200 jobs over three years would be increased by two-thirds and shoe-horned into the coming twelve months, resulting in the layoff of almost 20 percent of its workforce. As the evening wore on, news of unprecedented floods in Queensland, Australia, Brazil and Sri Lanka reinforced the multifaceted nature of challenges with which our species contends.

Aside from the emotion of despair, the theme of anger is not far from the conversations about the disconnected times in which we live. It would have been interesting for the traffic warden – who could not help himself from venting aloud his ire – to have spoken to my former student, who had a story to tell about the dealing floors on which she had worked and on whose paper-strewn boards she still craved to tread. The anger people feel about the injustice of ordinary working people helping to pay for the excesses of the privileged and unashamedly few is palpable. Blame, bordering on declared vengeance, was evident from the death threats made against the former head of the Royal Bank of Scotland, who fled the UK with his family in fear of his life while hanging on grimly to a multi million pound bonus, even after the government took a controlling stake in the bank to avoid economic catastrophe. The United States had its own sinister scapegoat in the guise of Bernard Madoff, who misled investors to part with millions leading eventually to his imprisonment.

Meanwhile, the Brazilian president blamed the 'white and blue-eyed' (*The Times*, 2009) for the global economic collapse, leaving the countries accused feeling awkward and unable to do more than emphasize the need for collaboration in such difficult times. Similarly, a Finnish inquiry into the banking crisis in Ireland described a society 'willing to let the good times roll' (*The Guardian*, 2011g), as well as targeting the banks for criticism. Fears for the consequences of a culture of blame have long been foretold. Within European nations, a shift to the political right has previously accompanied such troubles, as happened in the 1930s, for without the Great Depression, 'there would certainly have been no Hitler' (Hobsbawm, 1994, 92). Seventy years later there were warnings of likely electoral successes for political parties that propounded policies likely to appeal to extremes, including the British National Front, the French Nationalists and the US 'Tea Party'. Fortunately, no such shift to the far right registered itself in electoral terms, as widespread public discontent focused instead on governments of any persuasion, because they happened to be in power at the time of swingeing economic measures.

It seems that turbulent times have a knack for bringing out unhealthy extremes in human attitudes and behavior. As history shows, this is not a new phenomenon, but it is never too late to recognize the folly of reliance on extreme thinking, and perhaps we are starting to learn this lesson. However, despair, anxiety and anger are not surprising emotional reactions to economic crises, as individuals, organizations and countries struggle to come to terms with what went wrong and what the consequences mean for them. The next chapter will look at why an economic situation can give way to such animated or extreme emotional states, stemming as they do from not simply real-world events, but from the perceptions and expectations we hold. Whilst one could say that dissatisfaction and disappointment are the nursery slopes for an avalanche of negative emotions, it should be remembered that the human condition has so much to help it transcend such challenges.

CHAPTER 2

Why are these times so stressful?

The power of 'If'

Mismatched expectation is the enemy of happiness. Psychologically speaking, anything around which we anchor our existence can become such a core part of how we see the world that when it ceases to be, we experience loss and are left 'wandering'. At a personal level the reaction of grief to loss is a natural one and can have far-reaching effects on emotions and well-being as it affects our lives on many different levels. Most readily we can relate this to bereavement, to the break-up of a meaningful relationship and also to losing a job. However, we can also experience a lesser form of loss in our daily lives as disappointment or disillusionment when plans, communications or events do not go as well as expected. Indeed, we base our lives around assumptions about what we will be doing, about the expectations others have of us and those we have of ourselves. This could be termed a 'psychological contract', which is made up of an unwritten set of expectations existing between us and those who have a stake in these sets of expectations. Where either party fails to match these expectations, then there is the potential for unhappiness, disagreement and even poorer health. In the shifting environment created by uncertain economic times, there is far greater likelihood that our expectations will not be matched.

So why should mismatched expectations pose such a threat to the balance of our lives? What are the psychological mechanisms at work here? The answers are held within a mix of internal as well as external factors, which include our habitual style of dealing with events, long-standing aspects of our personality, the availability to us of social support from family, friends and colleagues, as well as the simple concept of how we spend our time. To a greater or lesser degree there are patterns to our lives: whether times of waking or sleeping, working or playing, we have 'routines' which shape our family lives, leisure and work time, holidays, and so forth. Some of these routines have been predetermined by forces beyond our control, such as nature (when it is light or dark), religion (holy days and practices), governments (statutory holidays) and organizations (working hours). However these routines do not simply impact on how we spend our time but, more importantly, from a psychological perspective they impact on how we think about and make sense of our lives. When any routine is challenged, then it is natural to expect some form of reaction. Turbulent economic times are ripe for such disruption. This chapter will explore the key psychological mechanisms which influence our personal responses, including features of our personality, our learned reactions to change and our perceptions of control. However, in order to understand our psychological response to economic turbulence, it is important firstly to examine the psychological contract which accompanies a materially based society and which often represents imperatives or 'needs' for many of its members.

The curse of 'affluenza'?

It has been argued by Oliver James that those living in Western, economically developed nations have been suffering with 'affluenza' – an almost contagious desire to shape our lives in relation to material possessions. The importance of such possessions can be determined by how much these are involved in our daily lives, any emotional attachment we may have formed to them, whether we have a choice about acquiring them and how others perceive them. These include our home – which we may share with others and/or which is where our possessions are housed – and perhaps our own mode of transport – a car or form of motorbike or bicycle – as well as items of personal and/or sentimental worth: clothes, mobile communications, jewelry, music, books, and so forth. Naturally, each of us relates slightly differently to material objects, but time spent looking at television or internet advertisements, in wandering around large shopping complexes, listening to the emphasis and status conferred on things, or how easily we are impressed/disgusted at others' possessions, all suggest that we live in a consumer society. The key messages which proliferate in such a social environment are clear: buying things will enhance your life. The rights and wrongs of such pronouncements are not for debate here, but what is crucial to understanding the impact of turbulent economic times is an understanding of how these pronouncements affect our collective mindset as a society and, therefore, what we actually do with our time.

By its very nature our species is social and has developed to exist in groups, as this has proved one key to our survival based on the basic principle, 'safety in numbers'. Our groups are of varying sizes, whether remote villages, sprawling cities, family-type units or virtual communities. To ensure the relatively smooth running of our lives in whichever grouping relates to us, social rules and conventions apply. Some are obvious and many are unwritten, but as humans we are usually quick to notice these and incorporate them into our behavior, so as not to stand out, or indeed apart, from our 'group'. The 'social animal' (Aronson, 1984) knows its survival is in some way linked to staying within the fold and will do things which may be surprising or even shocking to those outside that particular group. In this way, bankers' attitudes towards bonuses are accepted within financial circles as part of cultural norms, yet these assumptions contrast sharply with the wider public perceptions of massive payouts. Taking a different but everyday example, ownership of a car or van is seen as means of getting from one place to another and is actively encouraged by government incentives, workplaces and manufacturers, and is also viewed by many as a symbol of one's status in society. It is also about 'fitting in'. Without a car we can feel our options are limited, while ownership can confer an undefined, yet 'higher' status. In other words we feel the need to conform – at least to some degree – to remain part of the group and become successful within it. Ownership itself serves to affirm that we are who we want to be. It lies at the root of desire in many aspects of our lives and is a powerful psychological tool, of which the advertising and marketing sector is well aware.

Imagine now an existence tailored to servicing the desire to own things, which we may believe (and are often told) is necessary for successful and happy lives. Consider the time and personal resources of our daily lives devoted to such activity, perhaps over many years or even decades, for example in repaying the mortgage on a house. In the event of defaulting on a series of monthly payments we would run the risk of having it all taken away, perhaps not in a flash, but maybe over days and weeks as those from whom you borrowed come to collect on the debt you owe or as legal letters begin to arrive. How would our perceptions of our lives alter as opportunities for wealth-generating activity evaporate and with them the aspirations to own and keep homes, cars, electrical goods, and so forth? To ask such questions is not to suggest that life is all about possessions, but to highlight that for many of us such issues have achieved a very high priority. Unfortunately the mismatch between expectations and what is on offer has led to a grim battle for personal economic survival for increasing numbers of employed and unemployed people, and has become a much more widespread experience as a result of the economic troubles. In material terms, it is a harsh mismatch between what we have come to expect and a new uncertain reality which holds fewer guarantees. This is a psychological contract which we never signed, but instead have to get used to: one we have shaped and most likely shared with family, friends, colleagues, neighbors and even Internet acquaintances. In other words, with regard to possessions and commodities we have developed a set of unwritten expectations which we hope to see matched on a daily basis and which may well not be fulfilled. Where expectations are not met, individuals and their families risk a range of emotions ranging from dissatisfaction to resentment and even beyond to anger. If these emotions are mixed with a complete absence of control over the events which touch our lives, we have a potent emotional cocktail and no knowledge of whether the ensuing hangover has a cure.

Plan B – the lessons of Stoicism

In ancient history, the Stoics were those able to view life as though it were bound to turn bad at any time, or to recognize that it already had, and were prepared with a suitable mental approach to deal with such adversity. Marcus Aurelius, the Roman general and philosopher, was quite clear that in every day lay the prospect of more wrongdoing and that it was important to expect that, 'before night it will be your luck to meet with some busy-body, with some ungrateful, abusive fellow ... envious, or unsociable' (Zimmern, nd, 23). Studs Terkel, the American sociologist, whose 1972 book, *Working*, proclaimed that 'Work is about violence, to the spirit as well as to the body', suggests that in a modern context we can be well-served by not setting our expectations very high. A quick survey of pessimists we know tends to confirm that they see little point in anticipating too much from life if the end result is that one feels 'let down' or 'disillusioned'. This does not mean that the Stoical approach is the best for you, but it illustrates the point that raising the bar beyond what we can realistically achieve can be counterproductive if we start to beat ourselves up for not reaching or exceeding it. Obviously, nobody would want to dissuade either the young or old from aspiring to their dreams, as a number will actually achieve them, but for those who had not considered alternatives to success, the 'wake-up call' can be a troublesome reality. In that case, perhaps the Stoics would advise us to be forearmed with a fallback position if life does not match our ideals.

The notion of a psychological Plan B is not new, but the convincing and omnipresent consumerist message has left us with the notion that we do not need that plan. In other words, we are led to believe there will always be something we should buy, or we will always have reasons to earn money and somehow our personal economics will take care of themselves. This premise is undermined by recessions, as unemployment tends to soar dramatically and scores of individuals just like us cling on desperately in order to make ends meet. The importance of having a backup plan as insurance when the cycle of good times comes to an end is self-evident. It means we need to review everything in our portfolio of personal economic activities: home ownership, cars and holidays, home entertainment packages, energy suppliers, and so forth, in order to balance our personal finances. This need not be the end of our particular way of living and working as we know it – to take the view of the Stoics, the material world is something we can cut back on dramatically – but to leave ourselves without a psychological bolt hole is a very bad idea indeed. Therefore an integral part of any personal survival package in a recession is to assess our psychological portfolio, too. Where we prioritize our emotional needs and resources, we are more likely to find psychological health, security and happiness than when we are preoccupied with material gain or loss. The testimony of lottery winners tends to confirm this apparently homespun truism, but in the new reality which means struggling economies and cutbacks in spending, it is more essential than ever to take time to calculate the psychological resources at our disposal. In our newly configured personal balance sheet we will find featured our personality and style of behavior, our perceptions of control and sense of well-being and, perhaps, a newly shaped set of expectations which work for us, rather than for externally driven ideals.

What makes you tick?

The question 'what makes you tick?' is both alluring and threatening at the same time. It asks us to focus on 'me', which can be many people's favorite topic(!), yet requires an insight that we may not be accustomed to providing, even to ourselves. The modern study of personality charts a way through these perhaps unfamiliar waters, allowing us to identify key traits which we all possess to varying degrees. Decades of psychological research has attempted to distil the essence of our personality into fundamental patterns of behavior, resulting in the development of a 'Five Factor Model'. The theory suggests that we are located along a series of continua, from low to high, in relation to each of five essential traits (Costa and McCrae, 1992), namely:

- openness to experience – the desire to learn, willingness to take chances
- conscientiousness – keenness to work hard, being thorough
- extraversion – being outgoing and sociable
- agreeableness – likeable, eager to please, cooperative
- emotional stability – predictable, positively disposed, less troubled by worries

Clearly these are not the only facets of our personality, but are the five factors thought to be the umbrella terms for all those other adjectives which might be used to describe the way we are. The increasing use of personality testing in up to one third of job selection procedures (Leopold, 2002) suggests that whether we agree with such an approach to understanding ourselves or not, it can be useful to evaluate our trait profile. For example, when applying for a team leadership role would it be better to be described as relatively solitary and keen to go it alone or would we project ourselves as risk-taking and careless in pursuing a precision engineering or accounting job? The answers may seem obvious, but it is surprising how quick we are to give others an insight, yet sometimes struggle to provide our own assessment of ourselves. We are probably aware that we tend to deal with particular situations in a fairly consistent manner, but the details of this can vary between home and work life. For example, our ability to manage colleagues at work may be tremendous, but outside of work we might struggle to get cooperation from anyone in the family! When under pressure, the way in which we think and feel about the situation will either increase or decrease the stressful nature of what is going on. Therefore, it is not surprising that those who tend to have lower levels of emotional stability are more likely to struggle with major life events and conflicts (Williams et al., 2011). Furthermore, they are more likely to worry, either anticipating negative events or dwelling on past events, which in turn means they will spend more time exposed to the source of stress than someone who has higher levels of emotional stability. To compound matters, increased neuroticism is also linked with hostility, which could mean an individual will have less access to social support, as arguments are more prone to occur within close relationships (Baron et al., 2007). However there are four other major traits which mean how each is expressed by the individual is more complex than this. For example, higher levels of conscientiousness can temper lower emotional stability, while conscientiousness is associated with greater success in school and at work, in turn having a positive influence on one's socioeconomic status (Williams et al., 2011). Where there are lower levels of emotional stability, we are less inclined to engage with the problem we face as part of our coping response, whereas higher levels of openness to experience, conscientiousness, extraversion and agreeableness – along with age and the degree of challenge we face – predict our use of more direct strategies to repair a situation (Carver and Connor-Smith, 2010). While underlying personality traits are clues to our disposition, a fundamental role is played by the extent to which we see ourselves as able to express these traits. Self-efficacy refers to that perception and has been found as the link between personality and our experiences of stressors in the world around us (Ebstrup et al., 2011).

When it comes to understanding how we tick when faced with adversity, the concept of 'hardiness' has received considerable attention in personality research. This is equivalent to our resilience under fire and can be readily identified as a trait which enables us to cope effectively with a range of stressors, where otherwise we might succumb to poorer psychological health (Kobasa, 1979). A higher level of hardiness can, therefore, act as a psychological buffer against negative external events, such as looming unemployment. Essentially this is a cognitive appraisal system which determines our perception of threat and how to deal with it. Hardiness consists of three components:

- 'commitment', which reflects a feeling of worth for what one does and a proactive desire to get involved in things
- 'control', which suggests a perception of events as determined by the individual's efforts rather than by the environment around us (this is similar to the concept of locus of control which will be discussed below)
- 'challenge', which indicates we have a positive view of change, perhaps as a way of fulfilling our potential

Individuals who possess higher levels of each of these three components are less likely to suffer burnout, which is an extreme form of psychological strain (see Chapter 3). A study of nurses in both intensive and nonintensive care settings found lower levels of burnout in nurses with higher levels of hardiness (Keane, Ducette and Adler, 1985) and the risks to the mental health of combat soldiers is lower when their psychological resilience is stronger (McDermott, 2010).

So who is in control?

Perception of control over our lives is clearly a key factor in our evaluation of the world and how we survive life's challenges.

Rotter (1966) first publicized the concept of locus of control, which determines whether we see ourselves as mostly in command of events in our lives (internal locus of control) or as on the receiving end of what happens to be going on around us (external locus of control). Those who view themselves as key actors in their lives tend to use problem-solving approaches to 'make things happen', so that when facing difficult circumstances they are the ones attempting to get to grips with events and therefore have a greater chance of succeeding. Not surprisingly, their increased levels of coping and hardiness are linked with a better chance of survival. For example, hospital patients with an internal locus of control are more likely to be involved in their treatment (Powell, 1992) and are less likely to be depressed (Cvengros, Christensen and Lawton, 2005), while in educational settings 'internals' achieve better than 'externals' (Martinez, 1994). A large-scale study of immigrants found that those reporting an external locus of control were more likely to experience a range of negative health and social outcomes (Lerner, Kertes and Zilber, 2005). Naturally, there are many situations in which we do not have control over what is happening (for example, political and economic factors are beyond most individuals' ability to influence), however, the capacity to perceive some degree of control at some level is clearly important.

Positive outcomes for those individuals with an internal locus of control may be linked to their actually setting higher expectations for themselves and also attributing their success to their own actions, which in turn can provide a boost to self-esteem. It is possible to see positives and negatives in this approach, as failure to match expectations can also be demoralizing, and if one attributes results and outcomes to external factors there is less chance of feeling bad that it was because of something we did or did not do. Either way, in a range of scenarios the research shows greater success for those who see themselves as to some extent in charge of their destiny (Maltby, Day and Macaskill, 2010). Studies also tend to show the importance of the specific context in which both chance and the role of influential others, such as doctors and teachers, also can play a key part. This appears consistent with the popular ideas of 'making one's own luck' and 'it's who you know that counts', but making the effort to position oneself – both psychologically and physically – to take advantage of good fortune is entirely logical for surviving turbulent times. Naturally, we do not always feel that things are going our way, and our motivation to respond positively can be challenged, so it is not surprising that the habit of looking at events in a positive or negative light is highly relevant.

Case study 2.1   Optimism in the face of adversity

Ian has worked as an engineer for a multinational firm for many years. In fact, he was working there when he was diagnosed with cancer fifteen years ago. Since recovering, Ian and his wife Diane have seen their young family grow, with a daughter soon going to college and another at primary school. The news that a routine health screening had highlighted new problems for Ian reawakened old emotions and the discovery of a number of tumors threatened to knock the family's lives into a tailspin once again. However, Ian knew that he had beaten this once before and, strengthened by his unwavering optimism, the whole family began to feel that they could play an important part in his getting better if his operation went well. For Ian, the outcome was never in doubt: 'I have to beat this and I know I can'. For Diane and their daughters it was more difficult to be certain. Focusing on work and school was hard, but the sight of Ian still going to work and jogging or cycling to get fit for his operation reminded them of his determination, despite incredibly challenging circumstances, to live life as normally as possible. Ian's operation lasted seven hours and took two teams of surgeons to perform, yet within days he was out

$\rightarrow$

of hospital, already taking phone calls from work and even contemplating a short trip on his bike. To outsiders his recovery appeared nothing short of miraculous. Ian's positive outlook and Diane's endeavors to keep the family's feet on the ground – including hiding Ian's bike – meant that, as his recovery took hold, their lives could indeed carry on as normal. Occasionally, close friends would see their emotions come to the surface, but when asked how they had got through it all, Diane would modestly shrug her shoulders and Ian would beam, 'I knew I had to'. Their quiet strength and positive outlook was both remarkable and resilient, and after spending a short while in their company, seemed surprisingly normal.

Glass half full or half empty?

In everyday terms we are more likely to divide people around us into readily classifiable groups based on our outlook on life: on the one hand we find optimists – those demonstrating a positive approach – and on the other, pessimists – those more likely to behave in a manner consistent with neuroticism. Associated with the latter is a tendency to focus on the disadvantages and pitfalls of work, relationships, and so forth, such that these individuals can experience greater worry, lower moods, oversensitivity and lower self-esteem (Watson and Pennebaker, 1989). This means that the perception of strain by an individual who has high levels of negative affect is inflated and results in 'over-reporting' of symptoms of strain (known as 'the confound model') and can also mean the individual with high negative affect is simply more likely to succumb to strain when a source of pressure appears (known as 'the vulnerability model'). In extreme cases this can result in 'learned helplessness' wherein the individual feels that there is nothing they can do to alter a situation and this generalizes to other aspects of their lives, in future preventing them from acting to avert difficulties.

In complete contrast, positive affect reflects an enthusiastic and energized approach to life in general (Watson, Clark and Tellegen, 1988), so that people whose overall approach is highly positive will tend to view their situation more favorably than would even a slightly positive individual. The key to a more optimistic outlook can be learned, but may also be biologically determined. Martin Seligman – the father of modern positive psychology – suggests that the way in which we describe negative events can impact on how we think about them. If we look for the advantages in a setback situation and demonstrate what is known as a 'positive explanatory style', we are more likely to highlight the role of circumstances (rather than ourselves as 'failing'), and to consider that the problems are temporary (rather than permanent) and also specific (not likely to affect our life as a whole). This is more than positive thinking as it influences how we appraise the degree to which a situation contains the potential for threat, loss or challenge. For the optimist, the emphasis will be on the challenge component, as with hardiness, whereas the pessimist tends to focus on threat and loss. With this in mind, studies have revealed a number of surprising consequences of optimism: reduced distress after surgery (David, Montgomery and Bovbjerg, 2006), increased quality of life (Schou et al., 2005), more frequent exercise and reduced smoking (Steptoe et al., 2006), decreased likelihood of coronary heart disease and, even, experiencing longer life (Tindle et al., 2009). In attempting to explain the potential for such better outcomes, it is possible to highlight the associated contribution of positive mental health, the increased likelihood of seeking medical help and even the possibility of improved immune function (Maruta et al., 2000). The links between our physiological and psychological makeup are explored in more detail in the next chapter.

Great expectations?

'It was the best of times, it was the worst of times, it was the age of wisdom, it was the age of foolishness', sums up the paradoxes thrown up by a rapidly changing world. This opening to Charles Dickens' novel, *A Tale of Two Cities*, contrasts a violent and revolutionary Paris with a stable and prosperous London over two hundred years ago. The democratic traditions which followed the French Revolution and overthrow of a long-established and despotic regime have come to be considered as the lasting good from such times, but could not remove the bitterness of the accompanying savagery and loss of life. This is the paradox of dramatic change which, outside of war, revolution and environmental tragedy, is closely followed on a personal scale by the impact of disastrous economic times.

If we have become rooted in the traditions of a comparatively stable lifetime, the shift in our thinking in the wake of such upheaval is likely to be seismic. Those who have already experienced 'the slings and arrows of outrageous fortune' may either feel forearmed to deal with the impacts of change – almost like a psychological inoculation against future negative life events – or remain scarred by their previous experiences. Advocates of the use of *stress inoculation technique* (Meichenbaum, 1977) suggest that positive outcomes, particularly for those who have previously suffered physical or psychological trauma, can be seen as a result of providing prior training in how to deal with emotionally challenging situations. However, this type of planned intervention is quite different from situations of loss for which one is unprepared. Considerable research in social psychiatry has shown the potential time bomb which is the long-lasting effect of loss of, or separation from, a parent in childhood (Brown and Harris, 1978). The impact can be particularly damaging for an individual's self-esteem, both then and in later life. Researchers suggest that the legacy of loss is manifested in 'an inability to hold good thoughts about ourselves, our lives and those close to us' (Brown and Harris, 1978, 233), which in turn promotes a sense of helplessness affecting other aspects of our lives. When feelings of self-worth are lower, 'the individual is less likely to imagine herself [sic] emerging from her privation' (Brown and Harris, 1978, 235) and is troubled by 'an ongoing sense of insecurity and feelings of incompetence in controlling the good things of the world' (240). In itself this can predict decreased chances of having a confiding relationship with a partner in later life as well as the increased probability of developing depression. Therefore, when negative events occur in later life, the individual is already vulnerable. In Brown and Harris's large-scale study, 88 percent of adults newly diagnosed with depression had experienced a major life event which incorporated loss or disappointment. However, this pattern is not the case for all people who have experienced bereavement at an early age, although it is clearly important to configure the role of self-esteem and locus of control within these psychological processes. Nevertheless this model of reawakened personal challenges allows us to consider the potential impact of loss of employment and prolonged job insecurity on individual psychological health.

Clearly, past experience will color our perspectives and, in turn, our expectations in complex and deep-seated ways. So our psychological contract with the modern world is likely to be different in the details for all of us, yet there have been attempts by national and international governing bodies to set and standardize reasonable expectations. According to the Universal Declaration of Human Rights (General Assembly of the United Nations, 1948), everyone has the right:

- to work, to free choice of employment, to just and favourable conditions of work and to protection against unemployment (Article 23)
- to rest and leisure, including reasonable limitation of working hours and periodic holidays with pay (Article 24)
- to a standard of living adequate for the health and well-being of himself and of his family, including food, clothing, housing and medical care and necessary social services (Article 25)

This declaration represents a 'standard of achievement for all peoples and all nations' and urges that 'every individual and every organ of society...shall strive by teaching and education to promote respect for these rights and freedoms'. The challenge for individuals, organizations and governments is how to realize these rights when economic and political factors dictate otherwise. One politically motivated approach is to identify those rights which are open to compromise and those which are not. For example, in a recession governments might struggle to guarantee the contents of Article 23, but would argue that for those who do have jobs and for those who do not, Articles 24 and 25 should be applicable. Yet the notion of renegotiating such hard-won rights is likely to sit uneasily with the vast majority of people. So what expectations are likely to guide us in turbulent times? The following table suggests we may experience a changing psychological contract which departs from what we have known in times of stability:

Table 2.1   Our psychological contract in turbulent times

What individuals would like	What is likely to be available
Job security	More part-time and flexible working and fewer full-time permanent roles
Good standard of living	Decisions about priorities
Spare income to spend	Less flexibility in the household budget
Freedom of choice in work and public services	More 'forced' choices
To provide for family members	Reliance on wider family and community networks
Safety net for those in need	Maintenance of basic public provision

Amid this emerging picture of change are the blurred boundaries between home and work, the shifting tensions between private and public service provision and the increasingly opposing dynamics of what we would like to have and what we can have. The next chapter will examine how well we deal with such contrasting pressures which may exceed our personal resources to cope; in order to understand these better, however, it is worth identifying the economic, political and social contexts of change which is continuing to impact on our lives.

The challenge of change

There is no doubt that the economic recession which began late in the first decade of the twenty-first century is not the only motivator for change in our world. Certainly the economic upheaval has had an impact similar to that of a huge boulder dropped in the middle of a large pond with the consequences rippling to and fro. Of the approaches taken by numerous governments to survive the crisis, the prevalent strategy has been to shore up the banking sector by making huge loans to financial institutions and, commensurate with this, to cut back on public services and initiatives to balance the national accounts. As the initial incapacity of banks to lend money signaled the downfall of some long-established and many fragile businesses (see Chapter 1), the delayed effect of this rippling disaster is the announcement of many thousands of job cuts in the public sector. Workers in health, local government, social services, the armed services and law enforcement are in the front line to face job losses, joining the many in the construction, transportation and banking industries who were among the first victims of the economic freeze.

However, there are underlying drivers of change which form the background to these turbulent times, and these are a mixture of positives and negatives which affect our lives in different ways and to differing degrees. Increased life expectancy in more economically developed countries has provided nations with the new demographic challenge of caring for increasing numbers of elderly. For example, retirement ages have been reformed (in the UK and France), pensions cut (accompanied by national protests in France and Greece) and healthcare systems reformed with varying degrees of success (e.g., the United States). Additionally, the tightening of stances on immigration as well as the migration of workers have been in response to a range of demographic, economic and political considerations. For those already in relatively stable employment, there are issues of discrimination (e.g., gender, age, sexuality, disability, religion), employee rights (e.g., parental leave, temporary workers, the minimum wage) and organizational citizenship (e.g., job insecurity, bullying, employee engagement) which provide substantial challenges to individuals and groups as a matter of course. The massive leaps in technological innovation have revolutionized work so that we experience a 'waking week' rather than a working one (Parker et al., 2001) bringing with it a range of instant-accessibility issues, such as privacy, work–life balance and cognitive overload. The known and unknown challenges posed by environmental factors such as global warming and earthquakes, as well as the manmade threats of international terrorism add to the potent mix of unpredictability. Perhaps it is no surprise that there is an almost catastrophic tone evident in so many media news broadcasts and publications. Yet, despite all of this, as a species we are particularly resilient, having survived for many millennia. During this time we have adapted, migrated and grown as humankind. What is not known is how, in the long term, we are likely to respond to the speed of change in the modern era. It may take many centuries for our physiological characteristics to adapt to our highly technological environments, yet the enormous changes in the ways we live and work have demanded considerable adaptation in the last century alone. Perhaps it is no coincidence that global recognition of the phenomenon known as 'stress' – highlighted by a huge body of research since the 1970s – has been linked with human health and behavior, when the demands upon us have increasingly challenged our personal capacities to cope. Is this a strong indication that the world we have changed is doing so at a faster rate than that we can adapt to and that we are struggling to keep up? The next chapter examines what we experience as 'stress', both physically and psychologically, and how this is manifested in the turbulent times in which we live.

CHAPTER 3

The nature of stress in turbulent times

Since gaining popularity in the 1970s and 1980s, the concept 'stress' has achieved the status of an overused term. It is readily identifiable as a state of being which is usually less than desirable and describes our state of physical and psychological arousal when pressures bear down on both our daily existence and our sense of well-being. In the context of turbulent times, this is highly relevant to many of us. The first part of this chapter will clarify what is meant by stress, highlighting the emotional and bodily experiences which are consistent with it as well as the impact on organizations and individuals.

Defining 'stress'

We all have a working definition of the term 'stress' which we probably use to describe what is happening when pressure affects us. This is useful insofar as it helps us convey to others that things are not going well, but the meaning of the term reaches its limits when we want to describe anything more detailed that that. To complicate matters, 'stress' is often used to describe both the process of things 'not going well', as well as the outcomes for our health. To avoid potential confusion, we will refer to sources of pressure as 'stressors' and the consequences for our well-being as 'strain', including acute (short-lived) and chronic (long-term) outcomes. For a detailed history of the background to research into stress, the reader is referred to *Stress: A Brief History*, by Cary Cooper and Philip Dewe.

In order to set the largely negative experience of stress in context, it is worth recognizing that, for many of us, the existence of a spur to get the best out of ourselves, is sometimes a useful thing. In this way, a deadline might enhance our motivation to complete a task, or the presence of high levels of threat can contribute to improved performance in sporting or other contexts. In these situations it is as though the adrenaline rush which prepares us for action ('flight' or 'fight') is just what we need to reach our goal, and one can see the evolutionary purpose in these types of situations. However, if faced with such challenges on a daily basis and at a level we perceive as threatening, this can result in significant strain, both physically and psychologically. In other words, we are designed to withstand a certain level of real or perceived 'danger', but beyond that, stress can become a problem for our well-being and possibly for those around us, too.

Appraising threats

The starting point for any response to a demand in our environment – whether physical or psychological – is an appraisal of its relevance and significance to us. This process is fundamental to our survival and tends to shape our beliefs about an unfolding situation. For example, the first thought when our workplace announces the possibility of redundancies is likely to be, 'Will I still have a job?' This is a natural stage in assessing the level of threat we may be facing. Linked to this primary appraisal is a range of thoughts and accompanying emotions, varying from, 'I'm sure I'll be fine, as I do a good job and I'm too valuable to the organization', to 'Oh my God! How will I pay my mortgage?' How we respond to such a threat will also be determined by the psychological factors we bring to this scenario, such as personality, expectations, outlook on life and resilience (as discussed in Chapter 2).

Where our primary appraisal of threat concludes that this new situation is going to be a problem and an important one, we quickly begin to assess our potential reactions to the challenge. This process of secondary appraisal surveys the resources at our disposal. This entails survival as well as generating potential solutions and sources of support. In the insecure job scenario, we might seek clarification from the organization about the extent and timing of job cuts, so that we can identify the probability of being affected, as well as the timeframe for redundancies. Additionally, we might look for others as a shoulder to cry on and share feelings of hopelessness about the situation, or decide to protest by working less or not at all. We might join with others, either as colleagues and/or members of a union, to engage the employer in discussions to see if there are alternatives to staff cutbacks. This could involve examining the state of the business and exploring other opportunities to make the organization profitable. In addition, we might look at our own value to the workplace and see how to best present what we do, to justify continuing in the job. In this way, we might take steps to raise the profile of our good work and seek to make our skills invaluable to the employer. At a personal 'survival' level we might look for other job openings or a fallback position in case we do need to leave. This might mean devising or updating a curriculum vitae to show off our skills, personal qualities, experience and qualifications, ready to distribute if the need arises. Alternatively we might succumb to negative thoughts and begin to experience despair.

In short, the process of primary appraisal has consequences in itself and can naturally lead to a range of emotions and actions with the potential for both positive and negative outcomes. From a psychological perspective, the prospect of uncertainty is a particularly challenging one to face. It undermines our ability to assess the threat with which we are dealing as well as the resources we can rely on to help us cope. Perhaps it is surprising that research into the health of those facing job cuts and those who have already been unemployed for six months has shown that we can adjust better to joblessness than job insecurity. However this simply underlines the importance of understanding how we experience stress.

From well-being to strain

Bearing in mind the balance between what is good for us and what is not, it is worth considering both sides of the equation which feature well-being and stress. By viewing quality of life on a continuum which stretches from positive well-being at one end to strain and distress at the other, we can consider what we benefit from as well as what gives us pain in our lives. For example, positive well-being comprises feelings of happiness and satisfaction which play their own important part in our daily existence. At the other end of the continuum, poor psychological health indicates real impairment of functioning. By recognizing the presence and absence of positive and negative aspects of well-being, the spectrum of psychological health experiences may be highlighted (see Figure 3.1). The following subsections of this chapter consider each component in turn.

Good psychological health

In defining good psychological health, it makes good sense to emphasize the positives, although following a long era in psychology in which we have become adept at spotting the negatives, positive factors have not always readily come to the fore. What we call good mental health has been tentatively described as including 'an internal confidence of feeling and

Positive Well-Being			Negative Strain	
Good psychological health	Eustress	Stress/strain	Distress	Poor psychological health

Figure 3.1   A continuum of psychological health

knowing, an ability to make the fullest use of mental powers and abilities, and a capacity for enjoyment and self-content.' (Clare, 1980, 17). Other observers have taken a more structured viewpoint. Warr (1987, 1999, 2007), for example, has presented a five-factor model of mental health which includes the following:

- positive self-regard – viewing ourselves in a good light
- autonomy – the level of control we can exert over our lives
- aspiration – how keen we are to engage with our environment
- competence – how good we are at carrying out tasks inside and outside work
- integrated functioning – how effectively we coordinate these factors

It is worth bearing in mind that such an approach is Western in orientation. For example, within Chinese philosophy no model of mental health would be complete without the added feature of predetermined luck, which means a birth sign can influence the longevity of those born under it (Chang, 2007). It remains to be seen whether this operates in a similar manner to the role of optimism outlined in the previous chapter, although expectations are clearly shaped by cultural determinants. Taking all these factors into account, good psychological health may be defined as 'the state of well-being which draws upon our mood, abilities, self-esteem, customs, general disposition and our interpretation of internal and external events' (Weinberg and Cooper, 2007, 10).

As stated above, experiences of mental well-being can range between positive and negative extremes. However, if we wanted to risk a 'no-frills' definition, positive psychological health may simply mean feeling good about ourselves and what we are doing at a given time. This is not to say that determining the psychological health of an individual is a simple matter as everyone, after all, responds in their own individual psychological and physical manner. Yet, within the broadly understood limits of human capabilities and adaptability, we have developed ways to describe these responses. For example, Warr encourages us to recognize emotions ranging from pleasure to displeasure, from comfort to anxiety and from enthusiasm to depression. In identifying what accompanies and contributes to these feelings, we are more able to promote our knowledge and use of them for internal and external advantage. With this in mind a positive psychological state could be how we feel when relaxing in the spring sunshine, admiring the warm color of the yellow daffodils and the sound of birdsong – at this point, things may seem peaceful and our thoughts positive ones. In such a scenario, we might even dare to say we feel happy! However, such relaxing harmony with nature can seem a far cry from the reality of a hectic daily schedule and, of course, this example represents only one way of achieving a positive state of mind.

Eustress

A positive mental state is not only experienced in the process of relaxation, but also when we successfully rise up to meet the challenges of life. Far from admiring the wonders of nature, we might feel a different kind of 'buzz' from securing a victory or a sale against the odds, meeting a pressing important deadline or effectively navigating a difficult day's or week's commitments. This is close to the *eustress* described by Hans Selye (1956), in which we actively enjoy the challenge of life. This reflects the aspiration highlighted in Warr's model of mental health. Many people are suited to situations which involve personal challenge, an element of risk or higher stakes, and are more likely to be attracted to jobs which feature these aspects. For example, politics, stock broking, sales, advertising and entertainment tend to operate so that you are only as good as your last success. Cynics might argue that this is not too different from the daily experience of parenting, in which demands can be plentiful but the outcomes are hopefully more often rewarding. Certainly the element of challenge seems to get the best out of many of us and, in physical terms, it is well known that when we exercise the body releases natural chemicals associated with enhanced feelings of well-being. The action of such endogenous opioids suggests our bodies are designed to positively reward activity in psychological terms (Knechtle, 2004).

Stress or strain

Given the overuse of the term 'stress' and the potential to confuse 'stressful' outcomes with the 'stressful' process which leads to them, the term 'strain' is used here to identify the negative effects of experiencing high levels of psychological pressure on a regular basis. Strain suggests the cumulative toll resulting from exposure to daily pressures or the impact of a specific event. For example, the prospect of impending job cuts in a workplace, which continues over months as key decisions are made at higher levels of the organization, means that almost every day at work is overshadowed by uncertainty. Further along the process, the pressure created by having fewer colleagues working alongside us means our own workloads are higher than previously and we are required to work at an increased pace with less feeling of control over the job. Outside work, the closure of a childcare service might mean we are on daily alert to find new provision so we can be on time for work and avoid negative feedback at such unsettling times. Rising prices mean we cut back on leisure activities, which reduces our access to social support and ways of relaxing. In other words, stressors can build up to a point that we might feel we are accustomed to them but, curiously, we notice a new tendency to pick up minor infections, or to feel tired much more than usual. Perhaps others have found us more difficult to get along with than previously, and we make more mistakes in our work or at home. These are symptoms of strain which are considered in more detail later in this chapter.

In the hundred or so years since Sir William Ostler observed what he termed 'stress' in medical patients under his care, a range of physical and psychological theories has been proposed to understand our responses. These have included the relevant physiological mechanisms (Selye, 1956), our cognitive appraisal of events occurring around us (Lazarus and Folkman, 1984) and the importance of mismatch between individuals and their environments (French, Caplan and Harrison, 1982). The first of these approaches may well be more fixed than the others, while the second is more habitual, yet in turbulent times the relationship between individuals and what is going on around them is much more subject to strain.

Distress

In situations in which our almost daily exposure to stressors continues, or when we are faced with one or more major life events such as job loss and accompaning financial difficulties, the greater the challenge to our psychological and physiological coping mechanisms. It is possible that we all have our own 'breaking point' beyond which we feel we struggle to cope. The resources on which we draw may well help bring us back from that point, but where our ability to cope is impaired, distress is experienced. Partly depending on the continuing levels of our own internal and external sources of support, distress in the short or long term can lead to an episode of poor psychological health which may require some form of intervention.

Poor psychological health

One in four people experience some form of psychological health problem each year (Mental Health Foundation, 2011), with one in five of the workforce unwell at any given time (Royal College of Psychiatrists, 1995). In the UK the proportion reporting 'significant psychiatric symptoms' is higher for women (19.7 percent) than for men (12.5 percent) (McManus et al., 2009), although the numbers of people seeking help has increased significantly owing to government initiatives to widen access to psychological therapies (OPCS, 2002). As noted elsewhere (see Chapter 4), the prevalence of poor mental health in the UK is higher among the unemployed than those working full-time or part-time (OPCS, 1995). Little change has been noted in the overall prevalence figures for psychological ill health between 2000–07, which preceded the economic collapse (McManus et al., 2009). It is not surprising that surveys conducted since the recession began have indicated high symptom levels of depression and anxiety among 48–71 percent of those who have lost jobs, received pay cuts or had their working hours reduced, with the 18–30 age group hardest hit (*The Guardian* 2010b).

Psychological health problems comprise the largest group of health difficulties in the United Kingdom. One in six of the general population experience symptoms of strain which would merit diagnosis of a disorder such as depression and an additional similar proportion report symptoms linked to depression such as fatigue, sleep problems, worry and irritability (Black Report, 2008). While 20.5 percent of the working population actually report poor psychological health (Taylor et al., 2004), the proportion is higher than this among workers in unskilled manual jobs, and other occupational categories depending on which part, and these levels can depend on which part of the employment sector is being studied. For example the prevalence of mental ill health is much higher in parts of the UK public sector, such as health and social care (see Table 3.1). Surveys of psychological strain which have been carried out within public organizations during periods of major change have revealed high symptom levels among university lecturers worldwide (UK – Kinman and Jones, 2004; Australia – Winefield, Gillespie, Stough et al., 2003), general practitioners (UK – Cooper and Sutherland, 1992), civil servants (Finland – Vahtera et al., 2004; Japan – Nadaoka

Table 3.1 Prevalence of psychological strain among selected occupations and populations, expressed as a percentage of the respondents (measured via the General Health Questionnaire)

Authors	Country	Occupational group	Sample Size	Percentage with high levels of psychological strain
Nadaoka et al. (1997)	Japan	Civil servants	283	57.2%
Kinman & Jones (2004)	UK	University employees	1108	50%
Huxley et al. (2005)	UK	Social workers (mental health)	237	47%
Littlewood et al. (2003)	UK	Child psychiatrists	333	46%
Winefield et al. (2003)	Australia	University employees	296	43%
Weinberg and Cooper (2003)	UK	Members of Parliament (new)	66	29.9%
Nicot (2010)	France	Workers in the Central Region	6056	37.1% (men) 24.5% (women)
Wall, et al. (1997)	UK	Healthcare workers	11637	26.8–41%

et al., 1997) and even national politicians (UK – Weinberg and Cooper, 2003). A comparison between UK civil servants grouped by their job security status found that chronic insecurity meant the highest level of symptoms of strain, followed by those whose exposure to insecurity had been removed, while those who had not experienced any such job worries were in the best mental health (Ferrie et al., 2002).

The most commonly diagnosed psychological disorders are anxiety and depression, with the most frequent (mixed anxiety and depression) presenting among 9 percent of those with a mental health problem (Office for National Statistics, 2001; McManus et al., 2009). In situations in which a psychological disorder is present, the individual often finds it hard to cope with the demands of life inside and outside the workplace and will tend to be handicapped by high levels of psychological strain. The individual is likely to require help from a doctor, a counselor or the occupational health department at work, with many organizations buying into employee assistance programs which can provide twenty-four-hour telephone access for emotional support and advice (see Chapter 5). Where an individual is referred to a mental heath professional for an assessment, this will cover the range of symptoms, their severity and duration, as well as the degree to which daily life is impaired. Psychological help and/or medication may be offered depending on the outcomes of the assessment. The duration of absence from work due to poor psychological health averages 26.8 days (HSE, 2009), although clearly many people do begin to recover within this time period.

Symptoms of strain

Most of us can identify with the symptoms of strain but may not realize that the change in behavior we are seeing in others may be due to psychological challenges. Not surprisingly, we can be especially slow in recognizing symptoms in ourselves! While there is little doubt our experiences of symptoms of strain can be manifested differently between individuals, it is possible to divide these into the four categories described below: cognitive, behavioral, physiological and emotional.

Case study 3.1 Symptoms of strain in an uncertain workplace

Kemlash had worked for two years as a supervisor in the factory and, since his promotion, financial pressures at home had eased. His wife Sunita's main occupation was looking after their two young children, although she was hoping to get back into work once they were both of school age. What Kemlash had not felt able to share with Sunita was the decrease in orders his department had been receiving and the rumors which had been going round the workplace about possible layoffs. Increasingly, he was called

$\rightarrow$

---

upon by his team to give reassurances about the continuity of work at the factory, but much to his frustration Kemlash's senior managers were cautious in sharing any news. He had noticed he was having trouble getting to sleep and staying asleep at night. Worrying about work seemed to preoccupy his mind for most of the day and he no longer felt particularly hungry at mealtimes. Sunita had begun to ask if he was feeling all right, but Kemlash tended to brush her questions aside, preferring to play with the children, although not for very long. At work, he was finding it harder to focus on the tasks, and in between there were longer periods where there was not much for him or his team to do. Sunita decided it was time they had a proper talk about how her husband felt. After this, Kemlash realized his emotional state was affecting his work and home life too and decided to seek help from the doctor who helped him to manage his symptoms of strain.

Cognitive symptoms of strain

Our psychological capacity to carry out everyday activities involves information gathering, a good memory and concentration, as well as effective problem solving and decision making. Signs of cognitive strain, therefore, include impairment of some or all of these abilities, which in turn can generate negative beliefs about ourselves, other people or even certain situations, as we receive negative feedback about failure to carry out tasks and relevant duties. This can range from wondering why we keep forgetting things in the absence of any other explanation for doing so, to errors of judgment which cost the organization dear. Difficulties in concentration are common, as weighty issues distract our immediate attention, and the experience of mental overload can leave us feeling exhausted and unable to operate effectively.

It is not surprising that self-confidence can suffer during times of cognitive strain and the 'self-talk' which represents the thinking voice in our heads, can take a negative tone if we judge our abilities too harshly and worry too much about future performance. A study of hospital doctors' confidence in their performance of clinical tasks found that those with higher levels of distress reported lower levels of confidence in aspects of their work (Williams, Dale, Glucksman and Wellesley, 1997). Given the quantity of information some occupations are expected to retain and utilize, it is not surprising that overload can compound the problems facing individuals who have depleted psychological resources to deal with what is required.

It is not uncommon for an individual's attention to become fixed on specific ideas or events, which betrays anxieties about other aspects of the workplace. In this way, a focus on things which may appear trivial to others can actually mask worries about a much larger problem. Dealing with the smaller issue to the exclusion of other major problems suggests that the individual craves some level of control, which is understandable in a scenario of job insecurity or crisis, but doing so is not necessarily helpful if important decisions need to be reached. Turbulent times often present difficult challenges, and the heightened need for confident and competent decisions underlines the importance of consultation and, where practicable, time with others to consider valuable viewpoints. The development of guidance and protocols in advance of crisis situations also provides a helpful framework, giving organizations and their employees a head start in planning for processes and procedures in troubled times.

Physiological symptoms of strain

It seems entirely logical that the physical and psychological aspects of our well-being are positively linked, yet the traditional Western medical distinction between mental and physical health can tempt us into thinking that one is clearly separated from the other. Over one hundred years ago, the apparent paralysis of a South Wales coal miner's healthy leg, following the psychological trauma he suffered in a collapsed mineshaft (Eaves v Blaenclydach Colliery, 1909) was arguably one of the first recorded work-related cases of post-traumatic stress disorder, and it clearly demonstrated the relationship between psychological and physical difficulties. Over half a century ago, American cardiologists identified Type A syndrome as a pattern of behavior which resulted in coronary heart disease (Friedman and Rosenman, 1974). More recent research into psychosomatic medicine has underlined the many links between psychological problems and their manifestation in physical ill health, ranging from irritable bowel syndrome to psoriasis, and implicating life events and difficulties in the development of a wide range of unexplained medical symptoms (Guthrie, 2008).

What has been termed the human 'stress response' is an adaptation designed to enable 'flight or fight' as circumstances demand. This physical readiness to deal with stressors in either way has served the species well as a survival mechanism, yet the biological systems which underpin this are also activated by the psychosocial demands of modern living. Without an appropriate outlet, the repeated action of this age-old stress response can pose a threat to well-being (Clow, 2001). In the short-term, common physiological symptoms of strain include headaches, difficulty sleeping, indigestion, muscle trembling (such as a twitching eye), excessive perspiration, lack of appetite, sickness, shortness of breath, chest pain and even a decrease in sexual interest (Cooper, Sloan and Williams, 1988).

Over the longer term, chronic exposure to stressors and the experience of physical symptoms can lead to serious ill health. A European study of 6,467 pregnant women recorded an increased risk of premature birth among those working in an unsatisfactory job for more than forty-two hours per week (Saurel-Cubizolles et al., 2004). Increased workloads, as measured by the intensity of traffic on busy routes, was found to predict a doubling in coronary heart disease among 2,465 Danish bus drivers (Netterstrom and Juel, 1988). However, problems associated with extreme strain are particularly evident in the long working hours' culture of Japan, where there are already words in the language for death from overwork (*karoshi*) and also suicide due to overwork (*karojisatsu*).

Behavioral symptoms of strain

Our behavior when under strain is sometimes considered a measure of our resilience or even sheer stubbornness. However we may be feeling inside, our actions tend to be the thing on which others judge us. In this way, our performance at work and ability to 'take the strain' in uncertain or crisis situations are outward expressions of how we manage our internal emotional states. This does not mean there any right answers in doing so, and it is possible that many people will carry on regardless, but for some this may be because their ability to experience emotions is limited in the first place! ('How did that manager announce those firings in such a calm manner?') As the recipients of bad news we might prefer to see some display of genuine emotion ('At least we know they're human, too'.). Or we would rather people 'held it together' and stayed outwardly unmoved ('I wish they'd stop, or they'll start me crying, too'.). Whatever our preference, we cannot always be sure how much the behavior we see is reflecting how a person is feeling, as there is wide variation in how individuals both regulate and display their emotions. In addition, we may not know how people behave habitually and whether what we are seeing and hearing is their 'trait or state'. In other words, how much is their usual style of behavior and how much is a result of the situation.

There is one trait of behavior which has received considerable attention, has continued to hold popular appeal, and which has been linked with the development of strain and ill health. Type A behavior (Friedman and Rosenman, 1974) refers to a manner characterized by high levels of ambition, impatience, intolerance of others' perceived shortcomings, aggression and hostility and a general lack of insight into the impact of such behavior on others (Cooper and Bramwell, 1992). Research has suggested that individuals who habitually behave in this way are more likely to suffer coronary heart disease (Rosenman, Friedman, Straus et al., 1964). Although more recent large-scale findings have highlighted the primary role of alcohol intake and smoking in predicting heart disease (Sanderman, 1998), ongoing research has identified the important role of hostility in predicting serious ill health. In fact those with the highest levels of demonstrated hostility are more likely to develop coronary heart disease and cancer (Tindle et al., 2009). In highly competitive environments – and there are few in the world of work which are not – Type A behavior and hostility may be admired and encouraged as a way of ensuring 'things get done', and the toll on others subjected to unreasonable levels of either may be ignored. However, the longer-sighted business view needs to take into account the hidden human costs, which become measurable and compromise the bottom line when sickness absence, *presenteeism* (see below) and turnover rise and the reputation of the organization is damaged. Ambition is commendable, but recklessness feeds disaster. Arguably, the impetus for this book is the unbridled Type A behavior at the highest levels of the financial sector. For those who subscribe to this view, perhaps the justice many crave is provided by the potential psychological explanations for Type A syndrome. It is hard to know whether such a behavioral pattern stems from a need to exert control over one's surroundings in order to assuage persistent anxieties or from recognition that control is so elusive. The solitary coping strategies found by one study of Wall Street bankers suggests an air of resignation can result from such angst (James, 2007). Nevertheless, many individuals in all walks of life exhibit Type A behavior, and their risk of serious physical illness as a result of maintaining this approach to life is increased (Ursano et al., 2002).

Circumstances, as well as traits, can induce behaviors as a result of our emotions. For example, the feelings evoked by job insecurity or loss, major changes at work or financial worries are likely to impact on everyone sooner or later. People respond to different triggers at various stages in the unfolding processes brought about by change, and shifts from customary behavior can indicate that the individual is experiencing strain in some way. Presenteeism is recognized as one such response, in which employees feel that working longer hours and being visible at work from early till late, will of itself help to save their jobs. Very often this entails working while ill – physically or psychologically – and means that errors and miscommunications are more likely. Therefore, contrary to expectations, it does not mean that productivity is increased. In fact this 'impaired work efficiency' (Black Report, 2008) is responsible for double the costs accumulated by absenteeism (Sainsbury Centre for Mental Health, 2007; for discussion of both, see below).

Alongside presenteeism and absenteeism, emotional and behavioral symptoms of strain affect the quantity and quality of human interaction. Changes in behavioral timing, such as reduced punctuality, delays in communication, and procrastination can indicate individuals under pressure, as do avoidance and withdrawal from interaction with other people. The quality of social interaction may also suffer, such that irritation, anger and frustration with customers, clients and colleagues increase and rising numbers of complaints result. This also relates to incidences of bullying (see Chapter 4) which give rise to further distress.

Case study 3.2   When emotions boil over

The dashing of expectation is something we tend to adjust to, but the feeling of loss which comes with having to readjust a whole mindset is a much greater challenge. It is not surprising that the emotions which

$\rightarrow$

accompany extreme disappointment can be expressed in fairly extreme ways, especially when this is twinned with perceptions of humiliation. Many would not associate such loss in a sporting context, but the quotation from former Liverpool football manager Bill Shankly sums up a potentially forbidding mindset: 'Football is not a matter of life and death – it's more important than that'!

Much has been written about the reasons for violence around tense footballing occasions, but there appears to be an uncanny link between unmet expectations and the expression of extreme emotions by a small minority. The rioting by some River Plate fans after their team's relegation from Argentina's top division for the first time in 110 years led to street battles with police using tear gas and water cannon. In the aftermath, it was claimed that demand for antidepressant medication soared (*The Guardian*, 2011d). It is suggested by the Strathclyde police in Scotland that the frequency of domestic abuse incidents increases after derby matches between local rivals Celtic and Rangers, games that have also witnessed confrontations between members of the coaching staff, as well as between players on the field of play. In 2011, one such game led to the Scottish First Minister Alex Salmond convening a summit to deal with the issue.

Emotional symptoms of strain

The trading of emotions is inherent in our daily lives as we have dealings with others both inside and outside work. This is usual for most people, and is partly dependent on whether we feel up to handling the emotions of others or indeed our own. However, in turbulent times it is as though the emotional stakes have been raised. We become more acutely aware of the, not just actual but also potential, impact of others' emotions, as our 'survival' antennae more carefully patrol our environment for indications of threat. What did that line manager mean in the way he said, 'Things should be okay'? Or, 'Why does she look so down at the moment – is there something I should know?' To some extent the primary appraisals (see earlier in this chapter) we undertake are subject to overactivity, and this in itself can become draining.

The act of worrying is not traditionally viewed as a form of exercise which might make us feel as though we have run a half-marathon, but in a different way it can be just as demanding on our resources. Anxiety is, nevertheless, an emotional symptom of strain. In itself this can be debilitating over time and can become an episode of illness where the individual is feeling 'on edge', is preoccupied with worrying thoughts, finds it very hard to focus on other things or to relax and also suffers accompanying physical symptoms such as shakiness, palpitations, sweating and nausea. In common with a depressed mood, problems associated with sleep may be noticed as well as chronic tiredness. With a depressive episode, individuals also appear low in energy, seem disinterested in events (including things from which they would normally derive pleasure), convey an air of dejection and perhaps withdraw from or struggle with normal communications with others. The exact reasons for an individual experiencing the above symptoms are not always clear, as the relationship between cause and consequence can be complex, but the change in an employee's outward manner is often apparent to others. The employee's tolerance for challenging situations may be reduced along with levels of motivation, which makes challenging circumstances even more difficult to manage.

'Burnout' is the term often used to describe the extreme emotional strain seen in people-focused work, in which the daily trading of emotions can take a particular kind of toll. However, this term is not only relevant to job situations. Burnout consists of emotional exhaustion, depersonalization and a lack of personal accomplishment (Maslach and Jackson, 1986) and is applicable wherever there is ongoing demand on our emotional resources which we feel unable to meet. Emotional exhaustion is exactly what it says and refers to feeling 'used up', so that we can be left thinking, 'I have nothing left to give'. Lack of personal accomplishment describes the feeling that whatever activity in which we are engaged is no longer rewarding in the way we had previously thought: 'I used to love coming into work, but now I just hate it'. Depersonalization is perhaps the most unsettling of the three components of burnout as far as others are concerned. This reflects the individual's ceasing to treat others as they might normally, that is, with respect and consideration, and viewing them instead as units of demand on an already overloaded system. In this way burnout causes others to be seen as 'depersonalized', and they risk being treated uncivilly or without compassion, which of course is a serious problem at work or in lifestyles which depend on successful interactions and relationships with others.

Table 3.2   Potential symptoms of strain noticeable in stressful times*

Symptom	Very frequently	Frequently	Sometimes	Rarely	Never
Sleep problems					
Pains, e.g., headache, back					
Extreme variations in appetite					
Reduced self-confidence					
Difficulty in making decisions					
Problems concentrating					
Worrying more than usual					
Increased irritability					
Feeling miserable					
Withdrawing from contact					

*This represents a checklist and is not a diagnostic instrument, but by allocating scores of 4 (very frequently) to 0 (never), it is possible to loosely quantify experiences of psychological strain. Scores of 30–40 indicate high levels and may be attributable to ongoing circumstances in which the individual might benefit from seeking support. Scores of 20–29 indicate moderate strain which the individual should monitor to avoid escalation of these levels. Scores below 20 are likelier to be within the individual's coping capabilities.

The above section does not provide an exhaustive list of symptoms of strain, but it is subdivided to describe the range and variety of experiences of strain. These become problematic when the symptoms persist over time, although it is important to remember that these will vary between individuals and as relevant events unfold. However, it is not only individuals who experience strain, it is also evident in organizations.

Symptoms of strain in the workplace

Organizations are 'human creations' and as such reflect how their employees feel. Having identified ways in which individuals experience strain, it is important to recognize the symptoms which become apparent in the workplace. These refer to things which cannot be 'seen', such as absenteeism and turnover, as well as symptoms which are more obvious at work, such as presenteeism and low morale, but all of these have a negative impact on the functioning and performance of the organization.

Stress-related disorders have taken over from musculoskeletal difficulties as the leading cause of absenteeism from work (Cooper and Dewe, 2008). In the UK workplace, 40 percent of all absenteeism is attributed to psychological health problems, at a national cost of £8.4 billion (Sainsbury Centre for Mental Health, 2007). This is a proportion of the total 175 million working days lost through sickness absence due to all causes. The cost is £3.4 billion in the UK public sector alone, with employees off work for an average 8.5 days per year (CBI, AXA, 2006). In both Germany and the Netherlands, the cost of sickness absence due to poor psychological health has been estimated in the region of €3 billion (Houtman, 2005). Similarly, the toll of psychological strain related to work has also been calculated in the United States to cause up to 54 percent of all absenteeism (Elkin and Rosch, 1990) and, on the surface, it appears to cost American businesses billions of dollars (CCH Unscheduled Absence Survey, 2007). However, a study of lost working hours – rather than total days – among 54,274 US workers suggests that employees experiencing psychological strain tend to make up for lost time in order to maintain their job security (Hilton et al., 2009). It is also hard to ignore the social pressure which can build up on employees who have been absent for a long period – the UK average absence for a mental health problem is just under one month – and this may be felt more keenly by employees who have experienced anxiety and depression, as the response they face from colleagues can be negatively different from that towards a colleague recovering from physical illness (Glozier et al., 2006). Given the higher proportion of sickness absence due to psychological strain in people-oriented jobs, such as teaching, law enforcement, social work, nursing and the armed services (Seymour and Grove, 2005), this is an important issue which remains to be addressed.

According to the UK's National Institute for Clinical Excellence (NICE, 2009), 13 in every 1,000 employees quit work each year due to psychological ill health, with the accompanying replacement costs ranging between £3,150 to £9,000 depending on the type of job. The total cost of replacing employees who succumb to such strain is estimated at £2.4 billion annually (Sainsbury Centre for Mental Health, 2007). Although the average turnover rate due to ill health in the UK is as much as 18.1 percent (CBI/AXA, 2007), it is far higher in some public sector occupations because of additional job-related factors – up to 25 percent in social work (Huxley et al., 2005) and nursing (Scott, 2002) – often resulting in skills shortages. In the wake of such factors, the impact of forced cutbacks due to the recession is forecast to compound this problem.

Ever since the decline in job security in many sectors, presenteeism is increasingly recognized as an indication of behavioral strain. It describes a condition of 'impaired work efficiency' (Black Report, 2008), in which employees are unwell but continue to work, perhaps for fear of losing their jobs if they take sick leave. The result is increasing cost to the organization from reduced productivity – costs estimated to be as much as four or five times more than costs from absenteeism (Goetzel et al., 2004). In the UK presenteeism is estimated to cost as high as £15.1 billion annually (Sainsbury Centre for Mental Health, 2007) and as much as $44 billion in the United States. Among EU states, the lowest percentage of employees likely to work while sick are found in Poland (22.6 percent), Italy (23.5 percent) and Bulgaria (24.7 percent); while the highest percentage of employees who work while sick are in Montenegro (71.7), Slovenia (59.2 percent), Sweden (54.7 percent) and the United Kingdom (51.2 percent) (Eurofound, 2010). In the United States, the issue of decreased work performance was scrutinized in a study of 4,115 employees which projected that, on over 130 million working days each year, employees' performance was impaired by psychological and emotional strain (Kessler and Frank, 1997), with depression found to be the largest single cause of ill health among presentees (Kessler et al., 2001).

Organizational strain can also be seen in the negative impact on behaviors which are related to the job but not always essential for its conduct, such as social activities at work, voluntary overtime and attendance at training courses (Warr, 1999). Considered alongside the effects of working relationships under pressure, low morale, reduced commitment to the organization and the potential for increased error rates and complaints, the organization under strain faces considerable challenges to its well-being. Chapter 5 examines a range of methods for positively addressing a number of these issues.

CHAPTER 4

What do the sources of pressure mean to us?

This chapter examines three aspects of life affected by turbulent times and the psychological challenges which can follow from each aspect: namely, work, home life and finance. During the usual course of things, we can expect to face difficulties in each of these areas, but a common consequence of widespread economic, political or environmental change is that problems can arise simultaneously in more than one domain. This creates an increased likelihood that we will struggle with multiple demands across key aspects of our lives (see Figure 4.1). This is a bit like the physical phenomenon of

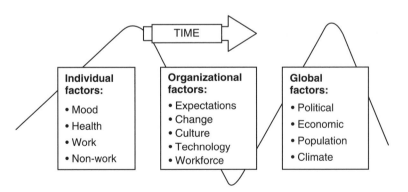

Figure 4.1   A resonance model of organizational stress in turbulent times

Source: From Weinberg, A., and C.L. Cooper (2011), 'The challenge of stress in modern organizations'; in R.J. Contrada and A. Baum (eds.) *Handbook of Stress Science: Biology, Psychology, and Health*, 151–66. New York: Springer (2010).

the impact of sound waves on a glass when they synchronize, so that greater and greater vibrations can eventually cause it to shatter. Hopefully, as humans we do not reach 'breaking point', but it can help to recognize where sources of pressure are coming from so that we can anticipate the potential impact and seek the best survival strategies before disaster strikes, even where there are no ideal solutions. By taking work, home life and finance in turn, this chapter will look at potential sources of pressure and the ways in which these can undermine our sense of well-being. The following chapters look at potential strategies for dealing with these challenges.

Pressure at work – psychological challenges to our well-being

As we saw in Chapter 3, psychological strain can manifest itself in a variety of ways at work, not just among individuals, but also in the organization which employs them. During times of turbulence in the economy, the effects can be become visible very quickly. Just how fast this happens can depend on the vulnerability of an organization to economic uncertainty, perhaps because it relies on predictable levels of consumer spending – such as the retail sector – or continued funding from large public bodies – such as government support for health and social services. The economic collapse of 2008 led to almost immediate effects in the banking, construction and automotive industry as organizations attempted to keep themselves afloat by ceasing spending or lending. In the longer term, as governments revised their plans, the impact on employees engaged in providing public services, such as law enforcement, health and education had become clear. In countries previously prosperous, yet hit hard by the recession, unemployment soared. In Spain 45 percent of the young people who were able to work were without employment in 2011; graduate unemployment in the United Kingdom doubled (*The Times*, 13 April 2011) and business experts forecast that 21 million US jobs would need to be created by 2020 to recover to the employment figures prior to the 2008–9 crash (McKinsey, 2011).

By highlighting the psychological challenges for employees in the uncertain workplace, it is possible to try to make sense of why organizations behave in particular ways and to anticipate how they may change in the longer term as things hopefully improve. In the meantime, innumerable questions are eating at the confidence of individuals considering their own futures in their current jobs: Am I indispensable? How long can I keep my job? Who can I trust to help me? Alongside these are keenly felt emotions fuelled by our reactions to what is going wrong. Some of these may be positive, but many will reflect negativity or indeed a sense of helplessness: for example, 'This is so unfair!' 'I have worked so hard and I do not deserve this!' 'I hate my employer; I detest the banks!' 'I simply don't know what is going to happen'. How these translate into everyday working life can be considered in two ways: firstly in terms of how the organization attempts to survive and, secondly, in relation to individual behavior at work.

Organizational behavior in the uncertain workplace

In thinking about how to balance finances, the reactions of the executive board or the head of an organization have some similarities to, and differences from, our own. There is the usual question of income and expenditures, and the recognition that costs are mounting and our ability to meet them is under threat. The instinct to cut back is obvious, and we are likely to be reminded of this by those around us, whether interested stakeholders or family members. However, the sheer size of a large workplace can provide options that differentiate the workplace from the small household. For example, if our organization is manufacturing large numbers of a valued item, such as food or clothing, or providing a service which is likely to remain in demand, such as healthcare or plumbing, then some may consider it possible to rationalize costs by improving efficiency, outsourcing, cutting back on some aspects of what is usually provided or expanding a success-ful product or service to increase revenue. There may even be limited scope for investment in an attempt to sow seeds for recovery further down the line. However, in businesses large and small, where a common outcome is reduction of current operations in some way, two of the psychological challenges which accompany this action are a) the knowledge that this can be painful for all involved and b) that it can be hard to foresee a bright future.

In organizations one of the less palatable realities of the reces-sion is bullying behavior. The prevalence of bullying in 'usual' times is shockingly high, with 25 percent of employees experi-encing this in a five-year period (Hoel, Cooper and Faragher, 2001) and considerable numbers witnessing acts of bullying, which also takes its own vicarious toll on them. However, the activation of the survival instinct in turbulent times carries its own agenda. In a climate characterized by the perception of cutting back, concern for fellow workers can be a relegated priority, often replaced by overtly selfish promotion of one's self. Phrases like 'dog eat dog', 'climbing on the backs of oth-ers' and 'corporate jungle' take on added significance.

Outsourcing and downsizing

Clearly each organization has its own characteristics and history which will in some way influence how it goes about the business of surviving turbulent times. For organizations which can count on the loyalty and resilience of most of their staff, cutting back on paid working hours, moving to part-time contracts and making cuts in wages might keep the business afloat. For others, the deficit in the budget may be too great to avoid job losses – temporary or permanent – or even closure. As highlighted in Chapter 1, the liquidation of businesses during the height of the recession did not seem to distinguish greatly between the large and the small, or between the old and the new. This pattern continued in the ensuring years; for example, in the summer of 2011 firms as diverse as UK train manufacturers Bombardier, home furnishers Habitat and do-it-yourself store Homebase hit the economic buffers. The psychological challenge of unemployment will be considered later in this chapter, but here it is worth examining the process and consequences of a planned reduction in the size of a workforce, either through outsourcing or downsizing. The words themselves are unemotional, suggesting on the face of it a deliberate reshaping of the way things are carried out. By outsourcing, organizations seek to transfer some of their functions to outside agencies, while downsizing refers to flattening the traditional structure of an organization built on layers, or hierarchies of management. Viewed in a more emotional sense, either of these means squashing some of the life out of the organization! The contrast between these anodyne-sounding terms and their real-life consequences could not be greater, but in an attempt to minimize the emotional connotations, terms like these are used in workplaces where cuts and efficiencies are being announced: 'We are reconfiguring or rationalizing our operations', 'redefining our corporate identity', 'reengineering our processes' or simply 'restructuring'. What can affect the psychological impact for all concerned – whether directly affected by proposed cuts or not – is the process by which this is carried out.

Outsourcing is one example of this type of restructuring whereby services are purchased from an outside agency or contractor, or part of the original organization is transferred to an external body to carry on the same work as previously done. For employees who are moved out to the new contractor as part of this transfer of business, the emotional outcomes are likely to be mixed: initial relief at keeping one's job, but then feeling 'let down, angry, uncertain about the future and a distinct lack of control' (Morgan, 2011), as changes are almost preordained in accordance with the transfer agreement. Of course, moving from one employer to another can carry advantages, particularly if not at all was well anyway.

However, if employees felt attached to their former workplace and colleagues, they are likely to experience a sense of loss, which is complicated by still having ties with them. In cases where the attachment to an employer was positive and strong, the employee may even feel that their identity as a worker is uncertain, too, and either begin to feel more distant from their work or to compensate by viewing himself/herself as a member or representative of their occupational or professional group instead (Morgan, 2011). It is this type of 'fragmentation' of work (Marchington et al., 2005) which removes a lot of the clarity from the employment situation for those who move as well as for those who stay. This recalculation of the job's parameters, which is quite different from losing the job altogether, raises a lot of questions for the individual employee. This ambiguity is mirrored at the organizational level as reaching final agreement over outsourcing arrangements or the transfer of departments as described above, can take much longer, with both sides seeking to minimize their risks. On the surface, at least, this can manifest itself as apparent mistrust, which in turn prolongs the process and compounds the uncertainty for employees in all parts of both organizations.

It is also vital to consider the impact of a downsizing initiative on the remaining workforce. The tendency for employers to content themselves with the thought that those who keep their jobs will be happy and healthier simply to have done so is rather blown away by large-scale research demonstrating the negative long-term impact on the health of employees who 'survive' the job cuts. A study during an economic recession of over 22,000 Finnish municipal workers who retained their jobs following downsizing in local councils has revealed that deaths due to cardiovascular disease doubled over the longer term and were increased by five times during the first four years after the job cuts (Vahtera et al., 2004). This type of finding lends weight to the idea of a 'survivor syndrome' experienced by those who hang on to their jobs, often with a mixed sensation of guilt for having done so and worry that they may not be long behind their former colleagues. This can result in negative outcomes for health as well as reduced commitment at work, with implications for absenteeism, productivity and mounting costs. Ndlovu and Parumasur's (2005) study of a South African automobile manufacturer found that, after downsizing, the damage to trust in the organization was universal across its workforce.

Key questions in considering cuts to working hours?

- How long will the shorter hours continue for? Is there an end date?
- Can I accept paid work elsewhere while under contract?
- How will the shorter hours affect my childcare costs?
- Am I eligible for additional support from the government?
- How might this affect any future redundancy payout or pension – will I still have the same entitlement as if I had remained full-time?
- Will my mortgage lender and utility suppliers accept reduced monthly payments?
- In the UK, earning less than half a week's pay for four weeks consecutively, or for six weeks in a 13-week block, means entitlement to a redundancy payment. (Osborne, 2009)

Redundancy

To read about the end of your job by email or hear it on the news is, to put it mildly, doubly inconsiderate. It is bad enough to learn that your job is at an end, either now or in the near future, but the manner in which this is conveyed stays with us for a long time. Despite decades of research into organizational life and management science, the desperation which grips those who administer this process too often seems to overturn collective wisdom in this regard. The email from the

UK Ministry of Defence instructing thirty-eight soldiers who had completed twenty-two years of service to 'start planning your resettlement' – including one serving in action in a war zone – sums up how wrong this process can be, and it rightly brought down criticism on the relevant government minister (*The Guardian*, 2011h). Similar accountability was not apparent for the board of high street retailer Woolworths, for many of whose employees news of liquidation was heard over the radio or on television as they were getting ready for work one morning.

Some debate whether or not it is better to announce job losses abruptly so that employees are not kept hanging on. After all, waiting can accrue its own weight of psychological pressure, and some skeptics argue that this time can offer employees increased opportunity to make life difficult for the organization. However, the European Union and the UK Health and Safety Executive directives on communicating impending change to the workforce suggests that the skeptics are out of step (Giga and Cooper, 2003). Levels of anxiety among a workforce inevitably rise as uncertainty rears its head, and it is essential that organizations pay heed to this because they are bound by law to maintain a 'duty of care' for employees' psychological and physical health, whatever the stage of the employment process.

The impact on employee well-being is real enough. The unexpected announcement of job cuts leads to an immediate increase in symptoms of poor psychological health, including anxiety and depression, which becomes progressively worse the longer the situation pertains. From a psychological standpoint, for many this is worse than unemployment, as after six months without a job they have had opportunities to adapt and develop coping strategies (Burcell, 2011). A Europe-wide study of 23,245 working individuals in 16 countries found that experience of ill health was up to twice as likely where job insecurity was faced and that this was unrelated to gender, age or education (Laszlo et al., 2010).

The news of impending job loss is rarely likely to be welcomed, yet organizations can take steps to prepare the way by keeping staff informed, making the process as transparent as possible and providing career and redeployment advice wherever practicable. The role and visibility of top-level managers are vital in showing that they are taking responsibility for the actions of the organization. This may carry challenges for them, particularly when greeting a potentially hostile audience, but having accepted a position of leadership this is an eventuality for which arguably they should be prepared and are presumably well-rewarded to face. Whether executives subsequently receive a substantial or larger than usual financial reward for their role should ideally be guided by human decency and sensitivity to the plight of the vast majority of less well-paid colleagues, but as events have shown, what actually happens may not always reflect these morals. In this regard, a host of bankers on both sides of the Atlantic have been targeted for their misreading of the unwritten code of workplace ethics. This has led to enquiries from both UK and US governments in 2009–10 and to a flurry of proposals for curtailing and taxing the bonuses awarded to bank employees. Less than a few years later, the value of bonuses paid to bank employees continued to run into the billions, with any decrease offset by increases in salaries of up to 40 percent (BBC News, 7 January, 2011).

It is clearly hard to maintain trust during a climate of uncertainty, yet paying attention to the issue of fairness – an issue uppermost in the employee's mind – is an important consideration in keeping people 'on board', and in treating with respect those who are leaving. Harking back to the 'psychological contract' described in Chapter 2, an organization is far more likely to maintain civil employee relations and be better positioned to help all employees (whether staying or going), by taking care to clarify its aims during periods of upheaval. It is challenging to retain a feeling of engagement among employees facing a period of notice, but the organization is more likely to match unwritten expectations if the end of a job is personally communicated in an unhurried and sensitive manner. This is especially the case in the light of a business plan which has already been shared with employees and is accompanied by evidence the employer cares sufficiently to advise or help individuals prepare for the next stage in their careers. This is not quite the theme of the employer in *Up in the Air*, the 2009 film in which George Clooney travels the United States as the hired 'firer', doing the work of the executives who cannot face the employees in person to tell them the bad news. However, what the film's plot seeks to show is that the human qualities needed in employer-employee interactions are too easily forgotten and considered disposable – just like the employees being fired by Clooney's character. In 2011 the British Psychological Society responded to the cost-cutting climate by running a workshop on how human resource managers can maintain appropriate exit strategies. Clearly, when the employer pays attention to the psychological contract by helping to create a new one rather than disregarding it, the impact of the outcome can only be better for all concerned, even though it represents a negative event. The perception of organizational support is recognized as a predictor of employee well-being (Rhoades and Eisenberger, 2002) in usual circumstances and, conversely, there is little to support the idea that serving notice of the end of someone's employment should entail humiliation or disrespect.

Individual behavior in the uncertain workplace

Understandably, the impact on the employee in an organization or a sector facing an uncertain future is likely to be one of anxiety. Having relatively little influence over outcomes often determined by factors beyond our control may, however, not be a new experience. Where these outcomes may bring about job loss, emotions can range from mild apprehension to absolute panic. Such feelings resonate across an entire organization and, consequently, some behaviors are more likely to come to the fore than others. These may represent the good – with groups of colleagues pulling together to offer mutual support and strengthen their productivity – or the bad, seeking to gain advantage at the expense of others. Equally possible is the abandonment of effective and safe working practices, which can endanger both health and performance.

Even outside turbulent times, the pressures of corporate competitiveness and political considerations have been implicated as contributing to transport and industrial accidents, yet these stand to be magnified in an economic recession. Even in the higher education sector, where psychological strain runs at exceedingly high levels, a harassed manager with a healthcare background exclaimed, 'We shouldn't be worrying about staff well-being when people are lucky to have jobs'. Six months later, due to ill health, she was obliged to change jobs and to reflect on the departmental culture she had engendered. Unfortunately, fear of failure and punishment is a common justification for ignoring tried and tested methods as some managers succumb to the pressure to deliver and cut corners in their dealings with employees under their supervision. Such short-sighted approaches only compromise the trust which is already under scrutiny in an uncertain climate, and this makes it several times more difficult for the organization to prepare for change.

Negative behaviors

Case study 4.1 Symptoms of a sick organization?

The arrival of a new departmental manager coincided with the announcement of major restructuring and efficiency savings. Across the organization staff members were already learning of their fate on overhead screens rather than in more personalized meetings, and the focus was now on the new manager's department. It was a

→

relief for the staff to know they would be kept informed and there were open meetings for colleagues to air and share their views. Yet, away from these, something else was happening which was not open and transparent and, in its own way, was far more damaging than the threat of projected cuts. Individuals who had spoken against the downsizing in open meetings were invited for one-to-one discussions with the new manager and told that their behavior would not be tolerated. In fact, he demanded apologies and written retractions and by now had surrounded himself with hard-nosed middle managers who did not question his behavior, which then became the norm for them, too. For nonmanagerial staff, the climate of uncertainty became tinged with fear. Worrying about their whispered discontent being overheard, they fell silent as managers stalked the corridors checking offices for those who were present, and indelicate emails were sent by the head of department to those who were not 'in favor', informing them that work roles had been withdrawn and replacement duties were now expected of them. By contrast, relatives of those who were within the 'circle' of top-level management were finding employment in the department, despite it being a time of cutbacks. Surely somebody would intervene? But who could concerned staff turn to in an organization which needed little invitation to let staff go? Nobody was quite sure how, but within eighteen months the restructuring had stabilized, the line manager was invited to accept another role and his accompanying middle managers were dispersed. There had been anger and resentment among ordinary staff that they had been put through this additional strain in turbulent times, but most of all their thoughts were with their colleagues who had been made physically or psychologically ill by the whole process. Eventually, the departmental manager became another statistic on the redundancy list.

Unfortunately, 'bullying' behaviors can take hold: unwarranted micromanaging, failing to consult individuals about changes affecting their jobs and even 'managing out' employees who object to the shifting norms. Naturally such tactics undermine psychological health (Hoel, Faragher and Cooper, 2004) and add tension to industrial relations. Clearly, organizations should take care to discourage such behavior, issuing or reinforcing clear guidelines to managers about expectations in such difficult times. The reverse scenario can also be the case as extreme dissatisfaction with a rapidly corroding psychological contract can result in employee behaviors tantamount to sabotage (Bordia et al., 2008). As lack of control is part of the psychological challenge employees face, it is natural that individuals try to take ownership over some aspects of their situation. However, in the absence of knowing how job insecurity may be resolved, or indeed knowing that one's job is coming to an end, what can the employee do to salvage a meaningful level of control? At one end of the spectrum it is likely that individuals will feel they are safeguarding their jobs by staying at work as many hours as possible, to emphasize that they should be viewed as indispensable. However, this contributes to presenteeism, which itself is indicative of psychological strain. At the other extreme sabotage, whether small- or large-scale, can represent its own threats to well-being, although organizations are more likely to expect unattributable Internet postings and petty theft.

Checklist of warning signs of an eroding psychological environment at work

- Employees working particularly long hours
- Culture of suspicion and blame
- Disrespectful communications between staff
- Increase in customer complaints
- Uncaring management style
- Mistakes, errors and accidents

Combating insecurity

Job insecurity is hard enough to combat without members of the organization 'compounding matters', and the questions posed earlier suggest that the psychological challenges of potential job loss relate as much to coming to terms with why this is happening as to how to cope. At one level, we may question ourselves and wonder how much of the job uncertainty is down to us as individuals and whether we are 'worth the job'. We may conclude that the answer will never be known, but it is important that individuals are discouraged from blaming themselves or each other and from questioning their ability where their skills are not the issue. Indeed, if the long-term offers little stability, is there the realistic possibility of providing employees with a suitable springboard to future employment by carrying out a time-limited project, which could serve as a positive advertisement for their skills? Alternatively, the answer to taking more control can lie within our ability to make clear what we already take for granted. This includes both our psychological resources and other sources of support at work, such as valued colleagues and friends. On the one hand we can take a step back and assess the positive aspects of what we have to offer, particularly our own skills and experience. This can help to boost our outlook as well as to prepare for a time when we may need to repackage ourselves to existing or new employers. It is surprising, particularly after longer periods of time in the same job, how we tend to view our work with an increased sense of, 'Well, anyone could do this, really', thereby undervaluing our own methods of working and the results these methods tend to produce. We easily forget that without a good degree of success, we would probably have been relieved of our duties long ago! We are also slow to acknowledge the significance of the extra acts of good citizenship we perform during our time at work, such as organizing social events, listening to others' problems or negotiating access to vital resources (even if this is replenishing the water cooler or photocopier!). While these acts are unlikely to feature on any formal job description, they contribute to the positive functioning of a working environment and constitute skills likely to appeal to prospective employers searching for supportive and emotionally intelligent individuals.

On the other hand, it is important to mobilize our own sources of emotional support. This can help us feel good about ourselves as well as create a much-needed sense of camaraderie for those sharing difficult times. If one person is worried about job prospects, then that person is never alone in having that anxiety. There are many positives to be gained from seeking affirmation from those you trust (taking care to identify them) that your skills have been valued by them, even if the organization can no longer realize your potential. This can give a renewed sense of purpose and a feeling that we have more control than we thought over what happens next in our lives. Organizations can also help by making it apparent to staff, managers and employees, alike, how to access advice and psychological support – either via employee assistance hotlines or in-house occupational health and counseling – which can benefit those struggling to come to terms with ongoing uncertainty.

The hardiest of individuals may even welcome the prospect of the end of the job as a source of positive challenge and an opportunity to escape a toxic work environment. Indeed, there are numerous examples of successful people whose opportunity to shine came from their ability to overcome adversity, without which they might have remained on a different and potentially unfulfilling career path. J.K. Rowling, after her first marriage broke down, went through a job change, from teaching English as a foreign language to ultimately finishing her novel about a young student attending Hogwarts school. Such examples provide inspiration to those facing the worse possible outcomes for their jobs by encouraging us to ask what do we really want from our working lives? However, this may not suit everyone's resilience level and, in Chapter 6 more detailed consideration is given to a range of coping strategies.

Beyond work – feeling the psychological pressure at home

Unlike organizations, we would hopefully not seek to rationalize the running of a household by cutting back on how many people are in it! However, the psychological difficulties facing families and households in which unemployment is a feature are particularly challenging. The support and resources available to the individual are obviously important, yet the strain on others in the household is likely to be experienced differently if the person is still adjusting to not having a job, has failed to adapt or indeed has given up hope of finding work. Rates of depression and other psychological health problems are almost double among unemployed people than in the general working population (DHSSPS, 2004). Notwithstanding the idea that moving out of a psychologically damaging work environment can be a relief to some, the impact of unemployment can be far-reaching, both in terms of how it feels and, more obviously, the practical considerations of daily living. Its corrosive impact on families and communities has been documented time and again (Black, 2008). This section will consider the psychological challenges experienced by the individual facing the prospect and reality of unemployment, as well as the difficulties endured by others in the same household.

The impact of not working

The timing of many jobs still tends to be 9–5, and so, one can gauge a lot about how well a location is faring by wandering its streets during these times. An increasing feature in Main Streets hit by the recession is the increased proportion of boarded-up shops and those which are run by charities, the numbers of healthy-looking individuals sitting on benches for long periods of time and the general sense of quiet. The local paper and television news carry reports of cost-saving schemes by the local authorities, including turning off street lights overnight, closing public toilets and cutting back on care activities for those in need. The local traffic warden or patrol officer is keen to tell you of plans to introduce evening parking charges where previously there were none and how early retirement looks much more attractive than it did two years ago, except that the changes to the pension plan mean it is worth less than before! Even outside the 9–5, the roads are less busy, as the price of gasoline further restricts movement and aspiration. Depending on where in the world you are observing or experiencing the phenomenon of economic downturn, the emotions are easy to read: There is a sense of anger and bitterness, of hopelessness and helplessness, and of waiting for things to improve. More closures or cutbacks are anticipated and the chances of gaining new permanent jobs seem a long way off. These realities burn deep into the psyche of the unemployed individual who wants to work and into the memories of a community.

The psychological challenges of unemployment

For every individual, psychological resources become much more important than before. There is more time to consider how the present situation came about and how the individual can overcome or even tolerate the very obvious challenges. Given the relevant concepts discussed in Chapter 2, it need not be all doom and gloom, but research highlights the overall negative psychological impact on well-being (see Chapter 3). By contrast there will be a smaller proportion of people who will feel liberated by the experience of reassessing their particular skills and ambitions, which could lead them on a more desirable path. However, for many there is the sense of urgency that financial considerations bring as families and households, landlords and mortgage lenders, as well as creditors, motivate a sometimes desperate search for sufficiently well-paid employment. This is not about pursuing a career dream, but surviving an economic nightmare. Assumptions which have underpinned one's working life cease to be. So what is the real nature of the psychological challenges which come with job insecurity and unemployment, and what can be done to manage the individual's experience of these? By identifying the personal difficulties in such situation, these can be more easily understood and, in the following chapters, a range of coping techniques is covered.

Among the first feelings about forced unemployment is the lack of control over what has happened and not knowing quite what to expect next. For most in this situation, it seems terribly unfair that the ending of so many jobs seems inextricably linked to the questionable performance of a relatively small number of overzealous individuals in the financial sector. There may be some consolation in realizing that nobody else seems to have control over what is going on either, but the key issue is one's own self-esteem: how do I feel about myself now that this happened? How one addresses this question partly rests on how much the job shapes your identity and defines you as a person. So much time can be taken up with thinking about work, let alone actually doing it in within a set number of hours, that it can feel like a habit from which one is rather suddenly withdrawn. In this way it is a little like the aftermath of the ending of a relationship: 'So I hear you and your job are not together any more' (!). As time goes by unemployment shakes the routines to which we were previously accustomed, as time is spent in other ways. Only the individual will know just how central the job was to their self-image and may therefore need to spend some time reflecting on the significance of their job loss. What remains is the significant factor which made doing that job possible: You!

The options of keeping busy or wallowing in self-pity may not be present, even if one feels like doing one or other. Yet, there remain the psychological challenges of viewing oneself in a positive light, securing another job, maintaining home life and relationships and of finding what to do with one's time to promote self-esteem rather than reduce it. The positive aspects of work are often readily transportable to everyday life, even if the financial rewards are not. Marie Jahoda pointed out the important role of structure in a working day, which is easily lost in a jobless situation, although sleeping late for the first few days is perhaps a welcome prospect, notwithstanding the tasks which are seen to by being at home! The promise of having things to do, as a result of advance planning, can feed into a more positive concept and combat a sense that 'I am not doing anything with my life right now'. Hopefully, activities will be linked to emerging leads for new work, perhaps generated by one's own searching, by local employment agencies, as well as by attending educational, skills or retraining courses.

There may be others who are glad to have you around at home – to a point at least (!) – and in the short term it may not be too unappealing to be without the psychological challenge of working. Weightier psychological challenges are more likely to arise as time passes without success in finding work. In addition to the financial strain that becomes an increasing feature of everyday life, there is the challenge to maintain a productive daily routine, to face the limits placed on social networks by remaining at home and the battle to maintain one's sense of purpose (DHSSPS, 2004). In this regard, knocks to self-esteem seem to come thick and fast as one is increasingly conscious of not being able to meet the expectations of partners, children, other family members and friends. While there are no easy answers to the practical aspects of earning money to maintain one's life as it had been, the need to maintain positive self-belief is clearly important. Playing a constructive role in reshaping one's own and others' expectations can be a frustrating business, just as it is for the human resource manager who struggles to be positive about company layoffs – unemployed 'wage-earners' face this challenge in relation to their own thoughts, as well as those of their families and close associates. Obviously, most people understand that ultimately the economic situation has brought this about, but this does not mean they are immune from the pressures of their own needs and wishes: 'Why can't we keep the car?' 'Isn't there some way we can get these things the children need?' 'Can't you come out for a drink?' It is often through one's family and friendship units that the potential limitations of the reality of unemployment are unwittingly reinforced.

Housing and home-life in turbulent times

One of the first visible signs of the economic freeze was the silence of the cranes which towered over building projects in cities around the world. The dramatic sight of these huge monsters of the construction industry coming to a halt signaled what might happen to the jobs of mortals working in their shadow. Even completed housing projects lay empty, from Dublin to Detroit, as ghostly monuments to an age of prosperity which rapidly evaporated. People sought to 'cut their cloth according to their means', they laid out new psychological contracts. This meant communicating to families and dependents that financial survival was the priority, no longer vacations, days out, new clothes and accessories or fashionable versions of this or that. To varying levels of success this was labeled what we would 'like' rather than what we 'need'. Rapidly rising gasoline prices in the UK led to half the drivers questioned in one national automobile survey cutting back on car trips (*The Guardian*, 2011f). However, where cutting back extends to having to give up one's home – mortgaged or rented – and especially if one's family is established there, this naturally gives rise to a host of difficult challenges. The number of housing repossessions by UK mortgage lenders stood at 40,000 in the year upto June 2011, which was over half of that witnessed during the peak of the recession of the early 1990s. A dramatic increase was forecast in the event of rising interest rates and mounting defaults (*The Guardian*, 2011e). The stagnation of house prices in the face of falling demand also increased the prospect of negative equity for new homeowners if prices began to decline. In this situation the value of a property could sink below its purchase price and saddle the owners with a financial obligation to remain there for however long an economic recovery might take.

If the situation of losing one's home has come about due to job loss, some degree of preparation can be possible due to working out a contractual period of notice, negotiating financial aid or getting time to find another job so that this does not become inevitable. In addition, some mortgage lenders are happy to consider 'forbearance and arrears support', provided all parties are aware of the risks of increasing financial dependence (*The Guardian*, 2011b). Reliable insurance against being unable to pay the cost of one's mortgage may prevent this scenario altogether. In the event of repossession, moving into temporary accommodations within the same locality may be an alternative – perhaps lodging with family or friends – provided of course it is possible to keep the household together. Relying on others to help in any of these ways, by lending money or sharing their property, can give rise to further challenges to our self-esteem, which can be moderated by agreeing carefully to terms, conditions and understandings, so that any agreement has less risk of turning sour. By placing such arrangements on a more formal footing, the potential emotional complications of guilt, future blame and resentment have a better chance of being avoided and things are more likely to feel like a two-sided, rather than one-sided, relationship. Underpinning the whole scenario of the loss of one's home is the need to ensure proper and impartial legal and debt management advice which can be obtained from organizations like the Citizen's Advice Bureau in the UK and Citizens Advice International in Poland and other parts of eastern Europe, as well Australia, New Zealand and also the Bronx in New York.

In the scenarios briefly mentioned here, the importance of social support is clear. Successful relationships underpin survival but, as experience tells us, these are the very things which can suffer greatly in turbulent times. By paying more careful attention to those close to us it may be possible to better understand how we and others are feeling and how much can be attributed to difficulty in dealing with the psychological challenges of the situation, rather than to a simple desire to end those relationships. Controlling one's emotions is among the most difficult aspects of dealing with unemployment and the injustices it promotes. Hopefully, our bonds with others are in good shape before we enter turbulent times but, independently of these, all relationships endure their ups and downs. Taking stock of mutual expectations and the nature of our relationships can help to set the scene for recovery, whether it is from loss of a job or a home. It can be surprisingly helpful to know at the earliest stage just how good or bad things are in relationships, otherwise we may be left wondering why things get even harder than anticipated and why sources of support we were hoping to rely upon seemed to evaporate. Individual levels of resilience shape how we and those around us react, but an understanding of everyone's emotions can increase our chances of addressing an already fragile situation, and of finding sources of emotional support as necessary.

Money and your mental health

Whether one faces unemployment or pay cuts, reduced pensions or insufficient income for whatever reason, the prospect of loans and debt are real enough. Managing changes in personal expenditure is something in which part or whole of the household may be engaged – perhaps through discussions sitting around a table with bank statements and pieces of paper with scribbled calculations. All of this is aimed at trying to make sense of the financial situation and what is likely to happen next. However, it can be a difficult prospect to do this, as there are many emotions and beliefs which can get in the way: 'It doesn't matter what we do, we're still in debt'. 'I can't see a way out of this'. Or, 'There's just no point'. In fact, the individual's perception of the severity of their money problems can have just as big an impact on psychological health as the actual level of debt (Fitch et al., 2009). It can be easy to succumb to the thought that nobody else having to deal with this situation has successfully battled their way out of it. It might be an unnerving thought, but most governments struggle with large debts and loans on a regular basis! Naturally, governments are usually large enough to cope, but the principle of financial survival is one that can apply to debts at all levels, whether household or global. It is not the existence of debt which is the problem, but how that debt is managed. At the level of the individual it can be too tempting to cease to monitor our money situation when we feel it is already hopeless, yet it is obvious that the bank keeps on counting and charging accordingly. Regular reckoning of household income and expenditure is important, no matter how uncomfortable an experience it proves to be. It can be helpful to take budgeting advice from reputable agencies (not moneylenders who charge high interest rates), or from trusted individuals who are used to dealing with money matters.

However, there is continuing temptation posed by the pressure to buy items for the family or the household, pressure which is compounded by almost every media outlet: online, mobile phones, television, radio and newspapers. Obviously there are some needs which really are needs rather than 'wishes', and going without them may not be an option. It can be tempting to enter into a rushed loan arrangement which turns out to be extremely costly in the long-term and may even carry a whole range of unpleasant consequences if the payments cannot be met. The significance of careful planning and working through possible scenarios requires the ability to control those emotions which suggest we should give way to pressure and perhaps accept what seems at the time the most convenient access to money. Admittedly, this is easier said than done, and there is likely to be that part of us which feels the need to take a gamble. Lotteries are an interesting example, as many feel that winning would be the magic answer to all our financial woes. However, there is a world of difference between buying a lottery ticket or investing large sums of borrowed money in ideas which have the odds stacked against them. In this regard, overoptimism actually can lead to further misery, so keeping a firm hold on what is probable is clearly important.

Planning for the future has been the advice of almost every prudent financial expert and, until the recession, pension plans were seen as a practical and worthwhile investment in future security. The good sense with which such schemes were viewed had meant that they merited little in the way of excitement. This was, of course, before a number of governments began to change the rules relating to retirement. In France and the United Kingdom, the pension age was raised, while in these countries and in Greece – as a condition for an economic bailout by other European nations – the benefits to be awarded by pension schemes were diminished. These actions prompted widespread civil discontent, leading to roadblocks and the detaining of a government representative by protesters in France, to the siege of government buildings in Athens and the promise of the biggest industrial action in the United Kingdom for almost a century. If tangible evidence was needed of the social shock caused by altering the expectations of whole populations, the changes to pensions provided it. However, for many, the more pressing priority was not that far ahead in the future – it was meeting the financial demands of today.

Where challenges to our mental health accompany financial problems, the difficulties can be multiplied, as our resources to cope and to make sound decisions are limited and without appropriate support we may be vulnerable to an even more unstable financial situation (Spinella, Yang and Lester, 2007). Research has shown that lone mothers are more likely to experience poor psychological health linked to financial strain (Cooper et al., 2008) and for men facing problems with housing payments the negative impact on their well-being can be greater than that of unemployment or losing a partner (Taylor, Pevalin and Todd, 2007). It is also recognized that people with existing mental health problems do not inform creditors or moneylenders of their health status for fear of stigma or embarrassment, and they potentially risk taking on an unwise loan which cannot be repaid due to health problems (Fitch, Hamilton, Basset and Davey, 2009). Additionally, where an individual without psychological health problems enters a debtor scenario, their chances of developing depression is doubled (Skapinakis et al., 2006).

There are a number of studies linking financial strain with a range of consequences for our personal identity, as well as our well-being. Where people are experiencing psychological strain related to debt, seeking help of the right sort is a significant issue. The behavior of banks in the years leading to the economic crunch of 2008 has not inspired confidence, causing the governor of the Bank of England, Mervyn King, to accuse them of continuing to capitalize on the naivety of the average consumer. Church elders joined the throng of critics, including the Bishop of Blackburn and Hyndburn in Lancashire, who described the recession as a 'kind of mini-death' in society, and the Archbishop of Canterbury, who accused the UK government of not doing enough to help those rendered helpless in such times. If any were needed, these conclusions confirmed the requirement for us to take far more personal responsibility and listen to sound advice in dealing with our finances, as trust even within the economic and social system is in short supply! The following chapters consider a range of strategies we might utilize in dealing with the challenges of turbulent times, starting with what can be done by organizations to help stabilize the uncertain workplace.

CHAPTER 5

Dealing with stress in the workplace: The options for organizations and their employees

Waiting for a miracle?

In turbulent times, we all need a survival kit, and the organization is no different from the individual in this regard. Whereas some organizations previously felt that the psychological well-being of its staff was either a given or a luxury, the full weight of taking for granted this aspect of our working lives has already become apparent. Those employers who have taken an active interest in their employees' psychological health will be in a far better position to withstand the stress of these times. Research has shown that in organizations in which workers feel engaged in their work, not only are profit margins better, in the first instance (Towers Perrin, 2006), but psychological strain is lower when staff perceive they are supported by their employers (Rhoades and Eisenberger, 2002). According to an annual report in *The Sunday Times*, 'The Top Companies to Work For' tend to be those which already integrate supportive management practices into the way they operate. Since having the support of your line manager is possibly the single most-important predictor of your mental health at work, then this support cannot be underestimated.

Clearly no amount of positive practice can hold back the potential devastation which the high tide of economic uncertainty can bring, but organizations did not start life fearing to get into the water. Furthermore, in these challenging times, it is not too late for an organization to grab hold of its own 'buoyancy aid'. The principles of good person-management are also those which underpin the psychological health of employees – it is no coincidence that these go hand in hand with increased chances of business survival and success. In the wake of the most recent economic collapse, Richard Lambert, the director general of the UK's Confederation of Business Industry (CBI), recognized that 'short-term returns may be lower, but the long-term rewards for management success will be a lot more sustainable and secure. ... In a more collaborative, less transactional world, closer relationships with customers, suppliers, employees and shareholders look like becoming the norm'. In other words, the adoption of a strategic approach which creates and enhances corporate citizenship is not just desirable, but absolutely necessary.

This chapter examines those aspects of the way we work which are key to employee well-being and require the attention of organizations in difficult and also not-so-difficult situations. It is no coincidence that the principles are those supported by research, over the last thirty years, into psychological health at work and, by facing the challenges which turbulent times bring, it is possible to bring about change which incorporates the flexibility to improve practices, empower staff and ensure clear communication. The outcomes are more likely to include higher levels of trust and productive behaviors than if organizations wait for an elusive business miracle.

Organizational approaches to well-being at work

There is nothing more likely to derail an emerging strategy than the timing of events, which is why incorporating good practice at the earliest opportunity is one key to survival. In this section those aspects of work most likely to influence employee well-being are examined, and reminders abound as to where these aspects have been forgotten. The news headlines on the day of writing this paragraph proclaim the UK government's new covenant with members of its armed forces, while another department of the same government predicts cuts in the numbers of serving personnel! The building of trust designed by one initiative is simultaneously wiped away by another. Clearly, it is only right to keep employees informed of what is going on, especially in difficult times, but the need for 'joined up' thinking is paramount. Below is the outline of a three-pronged approach to organizational health, which combines prevention, management and treatment options to tackle the immediate concerns of the day as well as to lay the foundations for a longer-term strategy for employee well-being.

This combination of organizational interventions provides a portfolio of employee-friendly options, which simultaneously benefit the organization:

- Primary interventions which focus on the *prevention of problems*: for example, considerate management and communication strategies during organizational change, participative job redesign, promoting organizational citizenship, management coaching
- Secondary interventions aim to *manage the symptoms of strain* and associated problems by targeting the individual in the workplace: for example, stress management programs such as relaxation techniques, stress management, assertiveness training, interview skills and job-seeking workshops
- Tertiary interventions are designed to *help the individual* who may need more specialized input to deal with the strain: for example, employee assistance programs offering counseling

Preventing stress in the workplace

According to the World Health Organization, 'a healthy working environment is one in which there is not only an absence of harmful conditions, but an abundance of health promoting ones' (Leka et al., 2007). This places the onus on the employer to be proactive in creating the best possible conditions for employees. Among the top 10 percent of companies earning a place in *The Sunday Times's* 'Best Companies to Work For', 94.9 percent of employees recognized that 'the leader of the organization runs this organization on sound moral principles' (*The Sunday Times*, 2009). This means that workers do look to top-level management to set the tone for how things are run, which clearly links to the culture and ways of working in any organization. As described in Chapter 4, the pressures on workplaces during a recession can manifest themselves in unhealthy behaviors 'across the board'. Therefore, it is no surprise that 'good leadership has the largest influence on employee engagement' (Bradon, 2009), which is defined as, 'a positive attitude held by the employee towards the organization and its goals' (Robinson, 2004, 408). As organizations need the support of their staff during downturns and upturns, it is important to recognize that those factors which influence employee engagement are also those which promote psychological well-being.

Key aspects of the workplace for the psychological health of employees

In the United Kingdom in 2004, the Health and Safety Executive (HSE), a government-appointed body, introduced its standards for managing stress to encourage 'a high level of health well-being and organizational performance' (HSE, 2009). These are examined in this section in more detail, but it is significant to note that among the key contributions to the uptake of the HSE guidance was support from top-level management for related initiatives. This not only under-lines the relevance of organizational leaders to the process, but also raises the prospect that many are less comfortable with psychological aspects of employee functioning than we might assume. In a review of an HSE advice service to small and medium-sized enterprises, less than 4 percent of calls and visits were linked to mental health at work (Tyers and Lucy, 2008), yet 40 percent of all sickness absence is due to psychological health problems (Sainsbury Centre for Mental Health, 2007). In the United States, the National Institute for Occupational Health and Safety has run its own research pro-gram since 1996 to support the dissemination of advice and research findings for organizations and employees.

The six psychosocial aspects of work highlighted by the UK's HSE as directly impacting on our well-being are:

1. **Demands** – this refers to employee workloads, patterns of work and the nature of the working environment, with an emphasis on whether staff members feel able to cope with the demands placed upon them. In the United Kingdom, HSE standards require that a system exist in the organi-zation to address concerns about workloads. It is recom-mended that employees are provided with 'adequate and achievable demands in relation to the agreed hours of work' and that their skills and abilities are matched to job demands.
2. **Control** – employees should 'have a say about the way they do their work' and 'where possible have control over their pace of work'. Consultation over working patterns and the timing of breaks is recommended, and opportunities to develop new skills should be supported.
3. **Support** – encouragement, information and sponsorship should be provided by the organization to its workers, enshrined in policies which make support by managers and colleagues the foundation for employee development and success. This should include constructive feedback and access to the necessary resources.

4. **Relationships** – positive behaviors should be complemented by policies and procedures for reporting and dealing with unacceptable behaviors in the workplace, such as bullying.
5. **Role** – employees should be clearly informed about their function(s) and should not be placed in a role in which performing a task causes conflict for those individuals. While this may be unavoidable in certain situations, systems should be in place to address 'role conflict'.
6. **Change** – this should involve engaging with and informing employees by providing opportunities for them to influence proposals for change. Employees should be made aware of the potential outcomes of the change process, and there is a responsibility for employers to provide training and support to help staff adjust. This may be particularly relevant during downsizing or restructuring prompted by an economic downturn. (HSE, 2009)

The first and last of these six recommendations are echoed in European Union directives which have set parameters for working hours and the communication of change initiatives to employees. The EU 'Working Time Directive' places a limit of forty-eight hours in a working week (taken as an average over sixteen weeks), although in some countries there is an opt-out clause which is intended as voluntary on the part of the employee. The European Parliament has also obliged employers to give advance notice of major organizational change in the wake of numerous examples of bad practice (Giga and Cooper, 2003). Employers could argue that workload and change are perhaps the two most difficult things for them to control in economically turbulent times. This highlights the importance of trust and flexibility between managers and workers. It is widely accepted that the future cannot be predicted with any great certainty, but it need not take much time to communicate updates on an unfolding situation and to open a window of opportunity for input from representatives of the relevant stakeholders, who include employees. The resolution in 2011 of the long-running British Airways dispute, which had dogged the company throughout the economic downturn, focused on the importance of two-way communication. The dispute typified the difficulties businesses face when there is a breakdown in communication (from whichever side) leading to disengagement and, in this instance, risked the loss of both revenue and reputation. By contrast, those UK companies that have been identified as the best to work for outperformed the FTSE 100 and reported 13 percent lower employee turnover, under half of the national average (Black Report, 2008). Similarly, in the United States a clear, positive relationship has been demonstrated between employee satisfaction and share value, with comparative market returns doubled for companies regarded by workers as the best employers (Edmans, 2008). In addition, the UK's Chartered Institute for Personnel Development (CIPD, 2006) claims that engaged employees take less sick leave, perform better, are more likely to recommend the organization they work for and are less likely to quit. Consistent with this, employee satisfaction with healthy workplace practices – staff involvement, training and development, recognition of work–life balance, health and safety – predict a range of business outcomes (Grawitch et al., 2007). The impact of fairness is also a consistent theme in relation to engagement, and considerable emphasis is placed on ensuring a employee 'voice' for key issues, providing opportunities for internal career progression, opportunities for varied work and fair pay (CIPD, 2009).

Sensitive to the potential yet to be realized in the workforce, the UK's Foresight Commission on Mental Health and Capital (2008) carried out a cost–benefit analysis identifying economic gains which could be made by taking an organizational approach to stress and well-being. Their initial projections highlighted huge benefits from auditing the psychological health of employees – in the order of £100 million per annum (National Institute for Clinical Excellence, 2009). This may seem surprising to many, but the act itself of assessing psychosocial aspects of the workplace is more likely to result in remedies to existing problems, either due to their recognition or to the political imperative that they can no longer be ignored! Beyond this, the Foresight Commission predicts that the implementation of strategies to prevent mental ill health at work would save £275 million. In the United Kingdom in the period 2008–09, three influential government-backed bodies drew together varied and credible evidence to inform recommendations which became public guidance for improving well-being in the workplace. Acknowledging the costs of employee mental health-related problems to individuals, organizations and businesses, the National Institute for Clinical Excellence (NICE) issued the following five recommendations for improving psychological health at work:

a) *Promotion of employee mental well-being*

Raising awareness of mental well-being (and similarly decreasing the stigma associated with psychological health problems) is an initiative which has gathered pace in the last twenty years. For some, the obstacles to considering this important part of our functioning have been attributed to simply not having any relevant knowledge or experience. 'Oh, that's just soft wishy-washy kind of stuff', suggests a stereotyping of the process which actually gives an insight into how we approach problems on a daily basis, as well as the factors which affect our performance. Nobody would doubt that we do face challenges and that there are times when we are better at tackling them. So where is the harm in actually considering how and why we fare the way we do in meeting our own and others' goals and expectations? The surge in interest in emotional intelligence suggests that we are moving towards a more positive view of those hidden processes which many have traditionally found difficult to verbalize. After all, as has been pointed out earlier, the costs of poor psychological health are certainly real, as are the benefits of acknowledging its importance, so there is little to be gained from skirting the issues it raises. Aside from the incidence of problems in employees' mental health, there is no denying there is, in organizations, also a political angle to raising this as a factor for debate. It will have occurred to more than one human resources (HR) manager that, 'If we recognize there is a problem, won't we be expected to do something about it?' Again, this is likely to be an unhelpful defense against inaction, as the law demands the provision of 'a safe system of work' and fulfillment of a 'duty of care' by the employer.

By considering the impact of policies and working practices on employees' psychological and physical needs, organizations stand to gain in many ways. There are many simple examples. In one study of UK railroad station managers who previously had their control withdrawn from reporting and addressing faults, restoration of their autonomy led to significant improvements in their well-being, while a comparable group of managers experienced increased psychological strain (Randall et al., 2005). This finding suggests that an appropriate prior assessment of the original change in practice might have saved the need for the withdrawal of this managerial function in the first place. In the remedied situation, not only were commitment and engagement likely to improve as employees realized their needs as 'whole' individuals were being taken into account, but the costs of mending inappropriate job design would have also been saved. Under these circumstances, the financial toll of recruitment, selection, training and appraisal is also likelier to fall. Naturally, it makes sense to ensure that the psychological issues addressed are those which are of relevance to a given occupational workplace, but above all this particular NICE recommendation addresses the need to promote 'a culture of participation, equality and fairness based on open communication and inclusion' (NICE, 8; Black Report, 2008). In another pertinent example, the training of manufacturing workers – who previously had to rely on technical support – led to their empowerment, which in turn paid considerable dividends. Increasing their level of control so that they could fix their machine tools led to a 6.3 percent increase in production time and additional output worth an estimated £125,000 (Leach et al., 2001). In a climate of change, such positive considerations also carry consequences for employees' physical health. Large-scale research involving 8,504 white-collar employees in Sweden has shown that where workers are involved in the change processes, rates of depression, coronary heart disease and absenteeism are half of those in circumstances where such participation does not happen (Karasek, 1990).

For a whole range of political reasons, simple steps which lead to improved psychological health may appear far easier in writing than to implement in practice, as 'Organizations are not simply mechanistic, they are subject to important psychological processes that influence the ways people manage their work relations' (Health Education Authority, 1997). In part this explains why interventions at the level of the organization are perhaps less commonly reported. Organizations are acutely aware of the image they project and how the announcement of an intervention may be viewed both internally and externally, as well as the potential impact if it proves less than obviously successful. However, in turbulent times, the far greater specter of business failure puts such considerations into perspective. With appropriate attention to planning, implementation and evaluation, which takes account of employees' mental health, there is a sounder economic basis for positive change to the psychological aspects of the working environment than persisting with a culture characterized by sickness absence, high staff turnover, burnout, presenteeism and suboptimal performance.

b) *Structured approach to assessing and monitoring employees' mental well-being*

As has been mentioned above, there are benefits to be gained from auditing the psychological health of the workforce, which could promote the identification of issues that need to be addressed and the recognition by employers and employees alike that it is a positive step towards improving the workplace for all. Statistics on sickness absence are perhaps the most obvious way in which to assess ill health and because of their objective nature, these are often the most cited measure. However, the reporting of psychological health problems is not without complications, as individuals may still be reluctant to declare that they have suffered in this way and general practitioners tend to use generic terms, such as 'stress' rather than a particular diagnostic term on notes verifying reasons for work absence.

The use of sickness statistics alone to assess well-being is limiting, as this focuses on where things are going wrong and then only if a period of leave results. As we have seen, presenteeism carries far greater costs. Similarly, staff turnover is indicative of an organization under pressure, but staff surveys have the potential to take the emotional pulse of those in work, whether feeling good or bad. Clearly, there are ethical issues to address, such as taking care to safeguard individual confidentiality and anonymity, as well as methodological challenges in ensuring the highest possible response rates to generate a representative view of the organization. These are in addition to selecting the right tools to reliably assess employees' experiences. The use of external agencies specialized in this type of activity is popular and, where conducted effectively, the issue of initial cost can be outweighted by savings to the employer in the longer term. For example, in the United Kingdom, a large-scale intervention which followed an audit carried out by Somerset County Council cost £510,000, but saved £4.2 million over three years. For small to medium-size enterprises, the costs of an audit alone are reduced commensurate with their size.

The widening provision of counseling and life-skills advice to workforces, often in the form of employee assistance programs (EAPs), is discussed later in this chapter, but it is important that employers make workers aware of their legal entitlements at work, as well as of their own responsibilities for their mental health. Organizations which are in a position to respond to the needs of staff at particular risk of work-related stress may feel much more comfortable in reassessing the impact on employees of working methods and external factors. However, the use of 'health circles' in German organizations – in which staff members meet specifically to identify workplace stressors – has been highlighted 'as an effective tool for the improvement of physical and psychosocial working conditions' (Aust and Ducki, 2004) because employees are probably better placed than anyone to pinpoint problems and suggest solutions for fixing them. Where such needs are identified, organizations can act quickly to ensure policies build on good practice and provide the necessary support at the earliest opportunity (see *d* below).

c) *Flexible working conditions*

According to the UK health advisory body, NICE, the economic benefits related to granting employee requests for flexible working hours are estimated to be in the realm of £165 million/year. Clearly, agreeing to these requests would be on the basis of mutual benefit, but such figures already tip the scales in favor of the organization. On the one hand, flexible working for employees, may also mean a more malleable style is required of supervisors and managers, but this is desirable, as are arrangements likely to improve employees' perceptions of control and 'promote engagement and job satisfaction' (NICE, 2009, 11). In the context of an uncertain economic outlook, the need for a more flexible working culture in this regard reflects the reality of an organizational approach to survival. Where this benefits both the organization and the individual, the 'win-win' is also reflected in the likely improvements to employee well-being.

At the interface between home and work life, the negative impact of stressors on psychological well-being is well-documented (Brough and O'Driscoll, 2005). This means that alternative work arrangements which offer employees flexibility – such as part-time work, job sharing, 'flexi-time' and working from home – are popular in themselves. In fact, the

UK Employment Act (2002) supports the right of employees with responsibilities to care for children and elders to request flexible working arrangements from their employer, requests which must be given consideration. The business case for meeting such requests is underpinned by the positive effects on workers' increased job satisfaction and improved family relationships (which clearly affect well-being at home and at work), as well as by improved profitability (Kinnunen et al., 2005). Organizations which operate with flexible working hours and arrangements and permit working from home benefit from below-average rates of absenteeism (Industrial Society, 2001) and increased quality of work (Kauffeld et al., 2004). Given that the level of support which employees perceive their organization provides is mediated by their line manager's approach, the approval of alternative work arrangements sends a clear message about the value placed on workers' personal and family lives (O'Driscoll et al., 2003).

d) *Supportive leadership style and management practices.*

The support of the line manager is the most-important predictor of psychological health among employees (Gilbreath and Benson, 2004; Shigemi et al., 2000; Weinberg and Creed, 2000). However, it is not always easy for managers to know the impact of their behavior on staff reporting directly to them, if for no other reason than those staff have a political justification for not expressing their dissatisfaction! Despite this, managers generally recognize the importance of their own interpersonal skills, as 76 percent indicate these are more significant for work outcomes than their role in authority (Worrall and Cooper, 2001). According to NICE, the manager's repertoire of communication skills should include 'participation, delegation, constructive feedback, mentoring and coaching[,]... respond[ing] with sensitivity to individual emotional concerns and symptoms of mental health problems' (NICE, 2009, 12). Managers' ability to motivate, train and support their staff is seen as a crucial factor in the mental health of workers, alongside the knowledge to refer individuals for appropriate sources of help, such as the organization's occupational health service.

The popularity of management coaching has increased hugely in recent years, with recognition that key aspects of behavior, such as those outlined above, can be assessed and enhanced. The starting point is often through 360-degree feedback, which establishes a baseline of the individual manager's behavior towards their own managers, colleagues, clients and direct reporting staff. Incorporating the behaviors highlighted by NICE, leadership and organizational qualities, communication skills, interpersonal sensitivity and resilience become the focus of the coaching process. There are positive benefits of such programs for managers and their staff alike. In a health service setting, training in 'creating a team environment', 'integrity and respect' and 'presenting and providing feedback' preceded improvements in both managers' and staff levels of well-being (Borrill et al., 1998). Similarly a case-control study of a coaching intervention in a university context found a decline in the psychological strain of participating managers (Weinberg, 2008). In addition, employees reporting to the managers in this study experienced increased satisfaction with personal development and job-promotion prospects, alongside reduced time conflict and fewer problems related to role change, all of which relate to organizational change scenarios. The promotion of individuals who possess the emotional strengths outlined here, alongside the necessary job-specific skills, would help to create and maintain a more productive climate in challenging times. The themes emerging from *The Sunday Times* 'Top 100 Companies' emphasize not simply striving towards common goals, but optimizing the process for reaching those goals. In other words, it is no longer enough to use any means to justify the ends, but to foster behavior which will elicit cooperation and collaboration. This type of adaptability is clearly essential where company survival is on the line.

e) *Support and advice for micro, small and medium-sized businesses (SMEs)*

As mentioned earlier in this chapter, the UK Health and Safety Executive highlighted the reticence SMEs can have in taking up advice about psychological health in the workplace and therefore in adopting an organizational approach to improve employee well-being (Tyers and Lucy, 2008). Depending on the size of a business, access to occupational health services may or may not be on-site, and this can determine the use and take-up of relevant support and initiatives. In addition, the responsibility in a small organization for health-related issues can be dissipated, yet the maxim remains true: 'Good health equals good business' (Black Report, 2008, 59). During an economic recession, the well-being of staff in SMEs is particularly vulnerable, as job security, rewards and social support networks are all under threat and so advice about preserving well-being could be of great benefit. In their favor, smaller organizations, including family-run businesses, may benefit from the existence of stronger bonds at the team level where perceptions of organizational support usually provide the link between experiencing psychological strain and intention to leave a job (Villanueva and Djurkovic, 2009).

Case study 5.1   Making tough choices in a supportive workplace

Peter Mather is head of Revenues and Benefits at one of the UK's largest metropolitan councils, which are responsible for the organization of local services. He leads over 100 staff whose task is to collect £300 million annually in business rates and council tax from the Greater Manchester borough of Trafford and to administer claims for housing benefit totaling £75 million. In

$\rightarrow$

the aftermath of the economic crash, Peter was seriously worried on two counts: firstly, over the anticipated funding cuts to his department – which he had expected to be a 'bloodbath' – and, secondly, how the staff would maintain the standards it had set in recent years. His team had recently won an award as one of the top three Revenues and Benefits Exchequer teams out of over 400 across the UK public sector.

The challenge was passed to Peter to save £1.2 million over two years in a way which would be sustainable in the longer term – a sum that amounted to savings of 35 percent of the department's annual budget. Peter informed staff from the outset that they would need to make efficiency savings and, rather than impose a situation upon them – and preferring a more people-oriented approach – he invited their views on how best to go about it. He had always been keen to engender an ethos of innovation without fear, which rewarded ideas based on sensible business plans and which recognized the efforts of his staff, such as articles in the monthly departmental newsletter and attending the annual awards ceremony in London. All staff were encouraged to contribute ideas and, not for the first time, Peter's style of participative management paid off. With 78 percent of all costs staff-related, the team set about generating ideas, using quality circles to consider optimizing their working methods, increasing the council's revenue base and reducing bad-debt provision. Peter noticed that staff motivation seemed to rise to the challenge, and levels of well-being actually appeared to increase, buoyed by Peter's stated commitment to minimize job losses, which was given additional credence by a policy of not recruiting new staff in such difficult times. A new policy for working from home was rolled out, and Peter met with those who came forward to negotiate flexible working arrangements which suited

→

them better. Whether working for the first half of the week only, or just mornings, staff were offered flexi-time and encouraged to produce a work–life balance which suited them. This could contribute to a 'win-win' scenario of a more satisfied workforce and also to sustainable savings on office overhead.

When Peter formally announced the final proposals for efficiency savings to the whole staff team, they knew what to expect. His policy of transparency meant he had not cocooned them and there were no surprises: out of over a hundred staff, only one person would be leaving, and then only through mutual consent. The union representatives and individual staff members came forward to thank him and the management team, showing genuine appreciation that the protection of jobs had been prioritized. Within the year came the answer to Peter's second concern: performance. The Trafford Exchequer team led all the Greater Manchester Authorities in its collections and also in benefit processing. If proof was needed, this showed that an open management style and flexible approaches to working could coexist with cutbacks and improved performance. In Peter's words, 'Authentic management does work and is effective in building relationships and developing a good team spirit. It is refreshing to see that an honest, flexible, participative management style approach can exist when cuts have to be made'.

Managing the symptoms of psychological strain in the workplace

It has been said that the 'sick individual is the symptom of a sick organization' (Carroll 1996), and if the previous section in this chapter was about preventing the development of problems in the workplace, this one is about dealing with the symptoms of sickness. It is not necessary that both approaches are mutually exclusive. In fact, it is far better to adopt a multi-pronged strategy, as structural changes to the workplace can take time, whereas moves to address symptoms and also to treat them can be instituted far more quickly. Therefore, it is not surprising that the most popular approach to tackling psychological and emotional strain in the workplace has been via 'stress management': the identification of symptoms of strain and the introduction of methods to help individual workers deal with them. These normally include workshops and initiatives which encompass a wide range of topics, including techniques designed to reduce physiological and psychological arousal levels – techniques such as relaxation, assertiveness training and improvement of communication skills. Stress management provision can be augmented in redundancy scenarios to cover employment survival skills, including job-seeking, interview and self-promotion skills as well as job-seeking techniques, as part of a package to help workers deal more effectively with the longer-term uncertainties of turbulent times.

Certainly, stress management offers help in a manner which is obvious for all to see and the costs of which are limited to a certain number of sessions, but employers run the risk of feeling falsely self-assured that their 'duty of care' is being fulfilled. An important drawback in this approach is that the onus for improving employee well-being could be seen as the responsibility of the individual – who may or may not attend and benefit from such activities – and not the organization. If this were the case, it would be possible for the organization to carry on in its usual manner and potentially relegate employee well-being to a far less-significant priority. The ideal lies somewhere in between, with both the organization and the individual taking responsibility for employee mental health. This reflects the importance of engaging staff as well as promoting recognition of psychological health in the workplace. If the organization provides stress management in the hope that it is an emotional 'Band-Aid' which will magically help heal underlying causes, this increases the risk of a worsening scenario. This part of a strategy for improving employee well-being is about the organization sponsoring the building and enhancement of workforce resilience and flexibility.

During the last quarter century, the stress management industry has boomed, achieving popular appeal in promoting skills designed to help employees cope with psychological and physiological indicators of strain, experienced as a result of facing stressful circumstances. These will be examined and evaluated in turn.

a) *Dealing with psychological symptoms of strain at work*

The first step in helping ourselves and others cope with psychological strain is to raise awareness of the symptoms. Workshops and websites form the basis for this type of educational approach to managing stress, as they inform employees about the warning signs and provide strategies at the individual level to improve coping skills (see Chapter 6). If we have increased awareness and understanding of how we think and feel in relation to dealing with others and events (Kagan et al., 1995), we are more likely to successfully handle these challenges. In turn, this introduces us to coping strategies which could be helpful when facing stress. The emphasis for such provision tends to be in work time and on work-related outcomes, yet stress management techniques can be employed outside of work time, too. Naturally, raising awareness is only part of the process of regulating the levels of strain experienced by the individual, and there is a wide range of interventions for which training can be provided by the organization.

A third of stress management interventions incorporate one or both of the most popular techniques, which are relaxation and cognitive–behavioral therapy (Giga et al., 2003). Relaxation focuses on psychological and physical methods of lowering arousal, whereas cognitive–behavioral techniques aim to modify the way in which we think about situations. Where more than approach is used, there is greater success in reducing symptoms, although when organizations face a choice, a cognitive–behavioral approach has been demonstrated as more effective (van der Klink et al., 2001). Whichever stress management package is supported, the aim is for the individual worker to enhance their ability to cope with occupational strain.

Relaxation techniques encourage the individual to focus on breathing and muscle relaxation, which can be used in times of acute pressure. Variations include progressive muscle relaxation (Jacobson, 1938), biofeedback and meditation. Meditation has been modified from transcendental techniques used in work settings (Benson, 1976, 1993) as it can be learned quickly and decreases physiological and emotional symptoms of strain (Murphy, 1996). Employees are encouraged to use this method in their own offices or in a nearby green space. In a different way, cognitive–behavioral methods aim to modify the way we think about situations, and there are variations of this technique which have been used with a number of occupational groups, including teachers, nurses and police officers (Freedy and Hobfoll, 1994). These techniques are designed to aid employees' capacity for accepting negative events without attempting to control them (Bond and Bunce, 2000). Rational–emotive therapy (Ellis, 1977) is one such approach which enables the individual to challenge irrational aspects of their thinking. This consists of interrupting the flow of anxiety-provoking thoughts and replacing them with more rational ones. For example, starting by tracing the individual's appraisal of threat in a situation (e.g., job cuts are on the way), to the worries this gives rise to ('It might be my job'), can help to identify emotional and behavioral consequences ('I'm so upset I'll stop putting effort into my work'). Rejecting the irrational aspects of these beliefs ('Doing something which gets me a disciplinary hearing will not help my job prospects here or elsewhere') can help to restructure the person's outlook in a positive way ('I'll keep working hard to ensure I get a good reference and also make sure I've got my eye open for new job opportunities').

It is recognized that well-designed programs can lead to reductions in psychological distress – including anxiety, depression and irritation – as well as improvements in physical symptoms of strain – such as muscle tension, blood pressure, heart rate and stress hormone levels (Murphy, 1996). However, there is little evidence to suggest that these changes continue in the longer term unless skills are updated from time to time. This again emphasizes the importance of using stress management as part of an overall strategy, to which the organization is committed, for reducing psychological strain in the workforce. AstraZeneca, which employs over 10,000 staff in the United Kingdom, established an in-house stress management program in 1988. Their winning a Unum Healthy Workplaces Award in 2007 confirmed the benefits of establishing and also maintaining good practice. With staff absence costs reduced by 8.5 percent (and accompanying savings of £1.2 million), the company also recognized benefits in staff outcomes, with 88 percent believing that AstraZeneca was committed to employee well-being. Also, 80 percent of the workforce reported that they enjoyed sufficient flexibility in balancing their work and home lives. In 2005, London Underground was similarly recognized for providing workers with access to a range of health-related skills training interventions, including relaxation, time management, decision making, work–life balance and managing relationships.

Research into the efficacy of individual stress management programs has provided variable results, which is perhaps not surprising given their different uses in various settings. However, studies have shown positive outcomes, from reducing burnout among mental health nurses (Ewers et al., 2002) to improving work performance among doctors (Michie and Sandhu, 1994). In addition, the latter produced the interesting, yet unexpected, emphasis on the 'opportunity to discuss their problems and getting collective support' (530). This underlines the importance of social support in the workplace and of creating an environment in which colleagues feel 'safe' confiding in one another and sharing strategies for dealing with challenges to their well-being. The pressures on time and space in many workplaces have spelled the demise of many a 'staff room', as financial drivers and the erosion of break times kick in. However, staff rooms are exactly the physical and emotional spaces employees need to unwind and draw on the social support of peers at work.

Formal training in communication skills is another popular method for combating the sources of psychological strain. It does not always produce the desired results, as often these results are not clearly defined or it is not known which relate to specific work situations. In contrast, the concept of coaching (see above) is a much more focused example which carries considerable promise. A related concept which is also enjoying a fast-growing reputation is emotional intelligence (EI) training. This is 'an ability to recognize the meanings of emotions and their relationships, and to reason and problem-solve on the basis of them' (Mayer, Caruso and Salovey, 1999, 267). Perhaps because of this, EI is linked to improved psychological health as well (Taylor, 1999); it is explored in more detail in Chapter 6.

Organizations are keen to exploit the possibilities which augmenting these interpersonal skills can create, so EI has the potential to benefit both the well-being of individuals but also contribute to achieving larger strategic goals. The introduction of a communications strategy at one UK hospital increased the potential for managers to meet and talk with the staff for whom they were responsible, extending to a policy to thank employees for their work: within two years, staff absence was almost halved, from 6 percent to 3.8 percent (HSE, 2005). Specific communication skills which commonly feature in workplace training include assertiveness training, time management and controlling Type A behavior. Given their transportability, these skills should also be considered within a battery of individual strategies for coping.

b) *Dealing with physiological symptoms of strain in the workplace*

Workplace health programs have achieved popularity in organizations, particularly in North America, where they aim to provide 'vigorous cardiovascular exercise, activities which promote muscle tone and flexibility, lifestyle counseling and fun and fellowship' (Dishman, 1988). As with other types of stress management programs, these claim to reduce the costs related to employee illness while improving productivity and maintaining good health. Although evaluation has been less than systematic, benefits have been found for both the physical and mental health of the employee, as well as the functioning of the organization (Voit, 2001). An employee fitness program at the ING bank in the Netherlands resulted in significantly reduced absenteeism for both regular and occasional participants (Kerr and Vos, 1993), while a study of automotive plants in Michigan established the cost-effectiveness and benefits of employee health and fitness schemes which provided both exercise options and follow-up counseling (Erfurt, Foote and Heirich, 1992). Nestle's commitment to the World Health Organization's guidelines saw it launch a 'Global Corporate Challenge' to encourage its staff to walk at least 10,000 steps each day. Their head of employee wellness, Dr David Batman, recognized that 'during the recession a lot of businesses are cutting back on these programs and people are worried about leaving the office, but we need these schemes more than ever'. Similar projects have seen high levels of employee engagement, averaging around 65 percent, ranging from health checks and smoking cessation to active travel to work (on foot or bicycle) and stair-climbing initiatives (Bull et al., 2008). Exeter City Council in the United Kingdom recorded a 20 percent drop in absenteeism after introducing a cycling pool for travel to and from work and arranging staff access to a gymnasium. Meanwhile the success of corporate initiatives, such as the 'STAYWELL' program at Control Data Corporation in the 1970s, was so successful it spawned a spin-off company which provides workplace health interventions to 12 million employees in the United States.

The combination of a growing proportion of sedentary jobs and the increase in stressors related to job insecurity presents its own risks to employee well-being in turbulent times. Estimates of increased chances of heart disease through a sedentary lifestyle vary, but its occurrence is almost twice as high in the inactive compared to active individuals (Berlin and Colditz, 1990). Physical inactivity represents a risk factor for coronary heart disease (CHD) along with the well-known problems caused by high blood pressure, high cholesterol levels and smoking (US Department of Health and Human Services, 1996).

In addition, the incidence of coronary heart disease appears directly related to the way people handle stress at work. A third of the effect of job stress on CHD among employees is due to its effect on health behaviors and stress chemical pathways (Chandola et al., 2008). A London-based study of 10,308 civil servants confirmed the link between work stress and Metabolic Syndrome, which is characterized by three of the following: elevated blood pressure, high-density lipo-protein cholesterol, glucose after fasting, triglycerides and abdominal obesity. Those exposed to chronic work strain (on three or more occasions) had more than twice the chances of developing Metabolic Syndrome than those who had not (Chandola, Brunner and Marmot, 2006). Taking the usual risk factors into account, job insecurity – along with work pressure and the individual's 'need for control' – was shown to predict CHD in a study of 416 middle-aged blue-collar workers over a six-year period (Siegrist et al., 1990). The good news is that changes in behavior can alter outcomes for the individual (Andersen, 2004). In fact, Australian economists projected that half an hour's daily walking for 5–7 days each week, by those able to do so, could lead to healthcare savings of AUS$126.73 million (Zheng, Ehrlich and Amin, 2009).

Helping the individual by treating distress in the workplace

Fortunately, in recent decades, attitudes towards psychological health problems have shifted with the realization that this aspect of our health is just as important as our physical well-being. It is no surprise that during challenging times, emotional distress is a far bigger problem than in other periods. The feelings of anxiety which pervade a workplace facing uncertainty and job losses are understandable, as is the sense of helplessness and negativity linked to potentially depressing situations. These can result in psychological ill health that can spill over into aspects of the way we work. Whether the individual takes sick leave or remains at work, the problems continue to be real for the organization which has a duty of care to all its employees. At the time of the Great Depression of the 1930s, Western Electric Company in the United States recognized the value of 'paying more attention to feelings and concerns' of workers (Lee and Gray, 1994, 218). As part of the company's research into productivity, interviews with 20,000 employees highlighted the relationships between the opportunity to express emotions about work and improved functioning as well as a decrease in tension (Arthur, 2000). Since the 1970s, there has been steady growth in similar initiatives. The most common is the Employee Assistance Programme (EAP), which provides counseling for individuals (and often their relatives, too) regarding both work-related and nonwork problems – including relationship difficulties, illness worries, redundancy or retirement concerns and financial worries. This service may be defined as 'the provision of brief psychological therapy for employees of an organization which is paid for by the employer' (McLeod and Henderson, 2003, 103). EAPs can be provided by phone or in person, and employees can usually refer themselves or be referred by a manager. It is important that users of these services can discuss, both inside and outside work, those factors which affect their well-being, a policy which fits with the common-sense view that we are the same people during working hours as outside them. Given the wide-ranging impact of the recession on workers, it is entirely logical that EAPs are able to support individuals in so many aspects of their lives and the number of such schemes has increased rapidly in recent years: 20–30 percent of the UK workforce has access to an EAP, and 99 percent of the service users are happy to recommend it to others (*Personnel Today*, 2008).

Levels of psychological distress among those self-referring for counseling through their workplace are very high, with 87 percent of respondents reporting close to maximum scores on the measurements used (Arthur, 2002). This study also found that prior to using an EAP, over three-quarters of employees felt their job performance was suffering and two-thirds would have taken sick leave if they had not had access to the service. Given the extremes of emotion with which individuals are contending, the potential value of such a scheme for employees and employers alike is clear. The average cost of EAP provision has halved in recent years to £14 per employee (*Personnel Today*, 2008) and although many more evaluation studies are needed, there is a consistent pattern of positive outcomes reported in those studies which have been conducted. Significant improvements following counseling have been seen in 60–75 percent of employees suffering with depression and anxiety (McLeod, 2001). Furthermore, 60 percent reductions in absenteeism have been recorded (McLeod, 2008), as has a decrease in the number of workplace accidents (McLeod, 2001), while an evaluation of Fortune 100 companies in the United States also noted improved job performance, workplace relationships and psychological health (Masi and Jacobson, 2003). An oft-cited cost–benefit analysis of the EAP at US firm McDonnell-Douglas, conducted by independent consultants over four years, collected comparative data before and after EAP implementation and demonstrated a $4 return for every dollar invested in the scheme (Alexander Consulting Group, 1989). In the United Kingdom, AstraZeneca saved the equivalent of £600,000 over ten years through its EAP, while Royal Mail made savings of £102,000 in six months through reduced absenteeism as a result of its own scheme (BACP, 2009).

For an EAP to be successful, a range of factors is necessary:

- Commitment at the top level of the organization
- Involvement of relevant stakeholders
- Clear policies and procedures
- Protection of employee confidentiality
- Effective publicity of services on offer
- Provision for follow-up of users of the service (Arthur, 2000)

Clearly, an effective EAP can serve a range of purposes; at one time, offering counseling to employees was considered likely to protect UK organizations from litigation in cases of psychological ill health that resulted from the workplace. However, more recent UK case law has made plain the legal necessity for employers to take a proactive approach in relation to mental health at work (Jenkins, 2010). Once again, this emphasizes the need for organizations to utilize strategies from across the range of approaches described in this chapter to prevent, manage and treat psychological problems in the workforce. Reliance on only one of these approaches is likely to leave both the individual psychologically vulnerable and the organization subject to its own ill health and poor functioning.

CHAPTER 6

Coping with turbulent times: A survival kit for the individual

Coping is the process by which we deal with emotional and practical problems, and it demands of us a range of skills and no little degree of flexibility. If psychological strain is someone's personal experience of these turbulent times and the individual's resources to deal with it are limited, how well is that person coping? Actually, this can be a pretty difficult question to answer, as there are few universal rules when it comes to coping! Perhaps it is hard to evaluate our ability to cope, as we may not have been in this situation before, or we may not know of anybody with whom to compare our situation. Whether or not this is the case, every circumstance (and individual) is different. Perhaps it is good enough if we can say to ourselves, 'I'm doing ok' or, if we are not, to recognize that 'Things aren't going well, and this is why'.

The reality is that there may be no right answers, and what works for some may not work for others. In this chapter, a range of approaches to coping with psychological strain are covered. Some approaches may suit and others not, but the key to successfully managing the impact of challenging times is to find something which does work. Having looked at organizational strategies in the previous chapter, here we focus on a range of coping methods reflecting physiological, emotional and behavioral needs. We also highlight personal strategies for facilitating positive outcomes, both in and out of the workplace. There are no guarantees of success, but as we have seen with organizations, awareness itself can lead to beneficial change.

'Coping is a shifting process' (Lazarus and Folkman, 1984, 142) showing that we respond to change in different ways at different times. This partly reflects the variation in the levels of control we have over an unfolding situation and, as we have seen in previous chapters, this also depends on our psychological, practical and social resources. As an everyday process, coping does not rely on the existence of turbulent times, but clearly is in greater demand during such periods of challenge. It is tempting to seek generalizations, but there is also a good argument for dealing with strategies on an emotion-by-emotion and problem-by-problem basis (e.g., Lazarus, 1993). For example, responding with anger to a text message announcing redundancies is understandable, but to react with such extreme frustration each time redundancies are discussed may not lead to the best outcomes. Although our conscious control over the optimal way to cope is limited, patterns of behavior which not only manage distress effectively, but also help to make the most of positive opportunities, are appealing.

Healthy versus unhealthy coping

Can there really be such a thing as unhealthy coping? It certainly raises a dilemma. In essence an unhealthy strategy could be considered a maladaptive one which ultimately exacerbates the problem at hand or, indeed, creates a new problem altogether. For example, the decision by an employee to refuse to cooperate with management's attempts to scale back a business – which refusal the individual may find satisfies their emotions in the short term – could result in disciplinary action which impacts negatively on that employee's subsequent search for a new job. However, if the individual's protest is one which helps to alter company policy and jobs are saved, who is to say that the individual was wrong to act in this way? In the latter scenario, things work out well for all concerned, but this dilemma is a little different from one in which the outcomes are likely to be poor come what may. For example, the decision to go home and turn one's back on work and on hope of ever finding another, or a different, job is not realistic if we aspire to reach the light at the end of the tunnel – unless of course that winning lottery ticket does turn up! There are a number of things which have somewhat higher probability than the one-in-fifteen-million chance of a gamble paying off.

However disenchanted they become with the world of work, many people cope in the first place by giving vent to their emotions. This does not always mean an outward expression of anger or disgust – witnessed or endured by others such as family, friends, colleagues or even enemies – but perhaps it is the ranting of a voice inside the head, like that produced by someone trapped in an enclosed space. One challenge is finding the acceptable expression of such uncomfortable experiences in a manner which does not cause distress to ourselves or others (Dewe, O'Driscoll & Cooper, 2010). Although we may not feel inclined to view the long term with any relish, we deserve a fresh opportunity: if we cannot start this process of emotional rebuilding, then it is unlikely that we will benefit from outside help. Categorizing methods of coping is an inexact science, so the following headings should be viewed as guiding rather than definite and the boundaries between them as permeable.

Building resilience – cognitive and emotion-focused approaches to improving well-being

In Chapter 2, a range of psychological resources was described which forms the basis for our ability to cope with challenging circumstances. This included the concept of hardiness, locus of control, positive and negative affect and self-esteem. Arising from the interaction between these mental resources and the world around us is a set of expectations of things to come, which in turn is inevitably reshaped in turbulent times. The psychological contract describes the unwritten expectations which guide our hopes and fears, and the idea that we need to reconfigure this is something to which we are becoming accustomed. 'Cutting our cloth' to suit our circumstances is one thing, but how easily this can be done is the issue which challenges our internal resources. Naturally, the level of difficulty is likely to be compounded by the situations of others close to us, who may depend on the success of our outlook and coping strategies. However, the first consideration – especially if others are looking to you to take the lead on things – is to be positive about your own abilities and, in short, to be good to yourself. (Palmer and Cooper, 2010). In economic terms this may seem a tall order when so much is outside our control, yet large-scale research has shown that maintaining a positive attitude predicts higher earnings (Mohanty, 2009).

Valuing yourself

Good feelings about oneself are often the things in short supply in challenging times, so hardiness and self-esteem are key psychological resources we need to nurture (Palmer, 1997). The loss of a job, or the prospect of that loss, are enough to rock self-belief. In turbulent times, it is easily forgotten that cutting back on jobs is not about the individuals and their skill levels, but reflects instead the position of the organization. In other words, it is not your fault if the job ceases to be. Even if you are tempted to sigh and say, 'Well why did they choose to cut my job?', the situation would likely not have arisen in the first place without the prevailing economic turbulence. Feelings of injustice and helplessness in the face of organizational uncertainty and cutbacks are understandable, but if looked at objectively, we would still understand these emotions if others were facing the same situation. This confirms that the circumstances are not about individual ability, but about the treatment of whole groups or sectors of employees. In short, it is both inaccurate and potentially damaging to attribute job loss through cutbacks to one's own actions in turbulent times. At the very least, this is one less reason to denigrate oneself and should be seen as a psychological pitfall to avoid.

The approach of putting potential negatives into perspective fits with the concept of hardiness (see also Chapter 2), which encompasses both the ability to value what we do and the desire to become engaged in what is going on. This approach stems from a level of self-belief, and positives which can help to engender this are certainly worth recognizing. Too often, we forget or do not register the significance of our actions, discarding them as 'part of my job' or 'because I'm supposed to do that', thereby failing to acknowledge that our own input made things happen. Perhaps this is one reason we feel hurt when those abilities are no longer required by an employer, because we realize that these do carry meaning for customers, clients, patients, and so forth, as well as for ourselves. Therefore, for all the more reason the knowledge, skills and abilities (KSAs) we use in everyday working life – and also, importantly, outside of work – are recorded and updated. Rather than awaiting an annual appraisal of what we do, which prioritizes the needs of the organization, it is worth itemizing job tasks for personal reasons. In this way, we can build a more accurate picture of what we do, which can result in being pleasantly surprised that 'I never realized how much I actually contribute' at work or, indeed, at home. The public justification given by former UK prime minister, Margaret Thatcher, for being 'qualified to run the country' was her self-assessment of having successfully juggled the running of a home. This does not mean we could, or would, wish to make such a claim, but it does underline the relevance of many skills which are too easily taken for granted.

Carrying out a self-appraisal exercise of our KSAs (see Table 6.1) is especially significant in uncertain times because the importance of maintaining an up-to-date curriculum vitae (CV) goes without saying. Even if a job feels relatively secure, the speed with which we can start looking for new opportunities may give us a valuable head-start if things do change. For all who need an eye-catching CV, there is an abundance of advice on self-presentation, from job centers to websites, but the inclination to undersell what we do remains. A common shortcoming with graduates is simply to state that they have a 'BSc (Hons) Discipline Name' and leave it at that, when what employers want to know is more about their work-related skills gleaned from undertaking types of study, work experience, research, and so forth. Very often it is not the specific subject, but the skills illustrated by performing effectively in a given area that makes the candidate attractive to an employer. In this way, an undergraduate with strong interpersonal skills can win out against those who seem more technically oriented to a particular job.

This reality is paralleled in many ways for graduate and non-graduate alike, where the transferability of personal skills is underestimated. Beyond that, people seeking work often forget, during interviews, to emphasize the value of their abilities in their previous organization, which should be an asset to any new one (Blackman, 2008). The same can be said about skills developed outside paid work, perhaps through voluntary, domestic or leisure activities. For this reason alone it is worth undertaking a job analysis of one's current or previous work/nonwork role to highlight the KSAs valued across many contexts. It does not matter whether we consider our role as purely home-based, work-oriented or linked to hobbies as diverse as photography, cookery or playing music, Table 6.1 encourages the reader to make explicit their job-related skills in daily life, both inside and outside work, which many of us take for granted and might consider too obvious to share with prospective employers. Whether currently in employment, managing a family or looking for work, the skills highlighted in Table 6.1 are those which appear on the wish-list of many employers, and candidates can turn this exercise to their advantage by articulating those skills.

Table 6.1   Making explicit the skills we take for granted

As part of my daily routine, I ...	Strongly agree	Agree	Disagree	Strongly disagree
communicate with others in person or by phone,				
advise others on how to solve problems,				
work well as part of a team,				
am willing to learn new skills,				
place value on how I deal with others,				
want to do my best,				
like to make a positive difference,				
have specialized knowledge/skills/ abilities in ...				

This exercise is not designed simply to boost self-belief, but it can also serve as the basis for a longer list acknowledging our KSAs. By placing value on what we do, we are more likely to tell others about it and this – much like a chance conversation – could lead to a promising opening. As Louis Pasteur, the discoverer of the method which makes milk safe to drink, remarked, 'Chance favors the prepared mind'.

Feeling in control

In line with nurturing a positive view of ourselves, activities which feed self-esteem rather than sap energy from it are especially important. Whether faced with an overwhelming set of demands or simply with the need to metaphorically pick oneself up from the floor, small things can assume a greater meaning than otherwise might be the case. This magnification can be turned to our advantage by making sure we do something, however small, which makes us feel good about ourselves. This might entail taking time to spend with someone who is positive about us for who we are – perhaps a family member or friend – or carrying out a task in which we normally do well or which makes a positive difference to our surroundings – both of which will also give us a sense of achievement.

For the sake of our self-esteem, it need not matter whether or not these activities are the ones we are supposed to do, just so long as they generate positive feedback for the view we have of ourselves. We can derive a lot of knowledge about ourselves from communications with others, so anything from making someone laugh to helping out by running an errand for them will generate good feelings about our capabilities. Similarly, cooking a meal, mowing the lawn, finding a good deal on the Internet or doing some form of exercise are all examples of things which we might be good at and which can make a positive difference. As any of these is the type of activity at which we might be accomplished, each provides the opportunity to say to ourselves, 'I can do this'. It not only serves to demonstrate a commitment to whoever may benefit from these actions, but also that we are proactive in wanting to make things happen.

In uncertain circumstances, this type of initiative-taking helps to shift the locus of control from around us to within us, so that we are the ones determining events rather than being on the receiving end of what the world has in store (Siegrist, 2009). This can also be reflected in the language we use to go over things that have happened, either in considering these ourselves or describing events to others. For example, our reaction is likely to contrast starkly on hearing someone say, 'I tried to do my best', compared with 'I wasn't able to do my best'. In both home life and the marketplace, where most roles carry responsibility and accountability, the way in which we deal with problems sends clear indications about how much we view ourselves as being able to influence events. Arguably, greater respect is earned by those who try to provide sensible direction or show a willingness to try and get things done, while those who give the impression of appearing uncertain, disinterested or helpless tend to be passed over for recognition.

The popular UK television program, 'The Apprentice', has shown that there is nowhere to hide in the selection process to find the next mover and shaker in Lord Sugar's business world, and on this program at least, fortune appears to favor those who contribute even if things go wrong. Research seems to bear this out, as candidates in job interviews who explained past behavior in terms of causes which they could have controlled attract higher ratings than those who do not (Silvester and Anderson, 2003).

How we view change

In the face of great change, 'many people have believed and still do believe ... they can't do anything about it and have no way of protecting themselves. As a result they may decide it's hardly worth making an effort and just leave events to chance. This attitude is more prevalent these days as a result of the huge changes we've witnessed and are still witnessing every day, things that no one could have predicted' (Parks, 2009). These words seem to sum up the approach of so many of us in these turbulent times. However, this quotation is five hundred years old! The sixteenth-century Italian icon of statecraft, Niccolo Machiavelli, certainly recognized the perils of change and their impact. Perhaps his words assume greater significance as we know he wrote *The Prince*, having been imprisoned and tortured on suspicion of conspiracy. His may provide an extreme example, but it remains a relevant illustration of resilience, nonetheless. He also wrote, 'It should be borne in mind that there is nothing more difficult to arrange, more doubtful of success, and more dangerous to carry through than initiating change[,] ... the innovator makes enemies of all those who prospered under the old order, and only lukewarm support is forthcoming from those who would prosper under the new' (Parks, 2009). For those who feel they are on the receiving end of change, there are crumbs of comfort in these words, too!

If we desire more than survival with dignity, by dodging the psychological pitfalls of turbulent times, we may need to view change as more of a positive opportunity rather than an indomitable threat. Resilience is certainly demonstrable via a sense of challenge as well as through aspiring to have a positive effect on things. It is linked in part to possession of either a largely positive or negative worldview. However, by giving ourselves time to consider a range of both good and not so good outcomes when facing change, it is possible to develop a focus on what can be achieved as well as on what might be lost. This does not mean that unwarranted and boundless optimism can always be the order of the day, but that a balanced focus on the potential advantages and disadvantages can carry an objective and weightier analysis of difficult situations. How this is conveyed to others sharing our circumstances is important for our own and others' levels of coping.

It may seem curious to consider that 'emotions can be caught by others' (Strazdins, 2002, 235), but in situations in which people identify over time with the feelings expressed around them, changes can occur in the way events and information are interpreted. In itself this can be useful or dysfunctional, but where it is the latter there are implications for our well-being (Strazdins, 2002). In other words, the ability to view challenge positively, if not actually embrace it, can be beneficial for developing individual resilience. A brief evaluation of the pluses and minuses of a new situation at work, or indeed any work situation, can help to objectify what might otherwise be an emotion-based reaction to change. As we shall see further on in this chapter, emotion can be a helpful guide to our gut reaction, but it is not always the companion to careful consideration of what to do next.

Through learning to see change via the perspective of how it could be useful to us, for example as a way to help us fulfill our potential, we can train ourselves to be less easily rattled by uncertainty – even if we decide that it is not a change we wish to stay around for. As Machiavelli and others since have observed, how willing people are to adapt to their circumstances is a key predictor of success; otherwise, 'When their approach suits the times, they're successful, and when it doesn't they're not' (Parks 2009, 101).

Rewriting the psychological contract

The set of unwritten expectations which govern our relationships with work, life and each other is rarely recorded for us to consider, let alone sign up to. As we have seen earlier (see Chapters 2 and 4) it is the nature of these expectations which gives rise to strong emotions. Changing times mean shifting expectations and a wider gulf between what we desire and what we are likely to get. This means that negative experiences of change can come thick and fast, perhaps becoming overwhelming unless we can capitalize on what we perceive as new opportunities. The advent of job loss or job insecurity encourages us to question the priority we have given to a particular organization or type of work. In such situations our loyalties and sensibilities are powerfully challenged and often reordered.

The need to provide for one's family and oneself takes over, so that working becomes more of a transaction than previously. Questions such as, 'Why have I bothered about this job?' or 'Why should I treat a job with respect when it does not reciprocate?' demand that we reassess what is important to us about work. Also, if we have to start again, what can we do which will suit us better, or where should we look to find widen our chances of doing something more rewarding or anything at all? This is where a proper and objective assessment of our own knowledge, skills and abilities helps – almost as though we could do with a career assessment similar to those at school, which may not have seemed so relevant at one time, but could prove really useful right now.

Job centers (open to the general public), career-advice offices (universities and colleges often support current and former students) and training and staff development departments (within employment organizations), are usually more than happy to offer relevant advice and training. The key step, which individuals who are under the emotional cosh of instability can find difficult, is to ask for this type of support. It is worth keeping in mind that an important part of building resilience is to supplement our range of skills and confidence in new or unfamiliar situations – seeking career advice is one in which we can reasonably expect positive feedback about ourselves and even the type of request we are making. After all, these services rely on people using them to ensure their own survival, too! Taking this step might even lead to updating our KSAs or to retraining to open up a new career.

During the writing of this book, I have come across an IT recruitment consultant who retrained as an electrician, a singer who requalified as a lecturer and a salesperson who became a driving instructor. On the surface, these career switches may not seem obvious, but, respectively, the use of technical, performance and interpersonal skills were common to their previous and new lines of work.

Ten positive beliefs about ourselves in relation to looking for work

- I have a range of knowledge, skills and abilities to offer
- There are things which I know I am good at, or at least others tell me I am
- Having the opportunity to show others what I can do will increase my chances of being successful
- Things may not feel fair right now, but this does not mean they will remain so
- People who have previously offered me work know what I can do and may be worth approaching in future for more opportunities or at least a reference
- I have been offered work before, so I am clearly employable
- I can access support from friends, acquaintances and services to help me

- Showing that I believe in myself will encourage others to believe in me, too
- I need to find the right person in an organization to ask about job opportunities
- It costs nothing to ask the question

One way in which we can rebalance the psychological contract where it feels unfair, is by altering the part of it which has to do with us. In the wake of the UK recession in the early 1990s, Herriot and Pemberton (1995) provided some very clear advice: 'Get out, get safe or get even'. In other words, it can pay in psychological terms to exercise whatever control we have in a situation to shape the workplace/home life 'deal' in our favor. In a company in which redundancies are indicated, we may not wait for the inevitable but seek to move sooner rather than later or, if the longer-term prospects are bleak, we might prepare our 'parachute' accordingly and forge good links with an alternative employer or prepare the ground for setting up our own enterprise. It could be said that those with a more cutthroat approach to personal relationships may take parallel steps. However, when it comes to the workplace – unless of course it is a family firm – we are not obliged to feel the same ties or loyalty. 'Getting safe' may take the form of learning skills which are unique and also vital to the organization, or in some other way adding value to the business operation. The ability to be up to date on the latest developments in any field tends to confer an advantage on employees who make it their aim to use it. Technological innovations are an obvious point, although these may not mean the job is done better, they can help to meet the expectations that work will be done quicker or in such a way as to impress those who may value the latest trends.

It is not only through honing a suitable exit strategy or making ourselves as indispensable as possible, that we can nudge the psychological contract back in our favor. Overshadowing the unwritten balancing act between what we want and what we get is the feeling that things should be fairer. Clearly such feelings are heightened where we feel there is injustice (Greenberg, 1987). In other words, 'getting even' can preoccupy our waking time as we may complain to anyone who will listen, or simply contemplate ways of 'getting our own back'. There are differences between how realistic or appropriate this aspect of rebalancing the psychological contract can be. For example, the denouement surrounding the involvement of the newspaper, *News of the World*, and News International, in phone hacking to obtain stories suggested that the public and its political representatives had had enough of this clear breach of trust. In July 2011, the UK Parliament voted in protest against the proposed purchase of a major television news channel by Rupert Murdoch's company, News International, and questions were asked on both sides of the Atlantic about the nature of this media organization's activities.

The 'tipping point' for opposition to doing business with News International was reached after the allegation that the *News of the World* had employed the services of an individual who hacked into the phones of public figures and people in the news, including a murdered schoolgirl. It was claimed the operative had deleted messages from her phone at the time police and her family were searching for her. The widespread outrage and condemnation resulting from clear violation of expectations of media behaviour led to the closure of the newspaper within days of the scandal breaking. This appears to be an extreme example, but it illustrates that 'getting even' with wrongdoing is a necessary step in accountability and, hopefully, changing things thereafter for the better.

The discovery of the cover-up, which preceded the disclosure of what had happened in this and other comparable cases, necessitated reconsideration of the relationship between key aspects of the UK establishment – politicians, law enforcement and the media. In this sense, turbulence in the sectors involved was both desirable and essential. However, at the level of the individual employee, disgruntled by the behavior of the employer – such as journalists who objected to unethical practices in newspaper reporting – the path to justice was much more treacherous, as being in the minority and swimming against the tide created vulnerability. This was highlighted by *Private Eye* magazine, which devoted a special issue to UK healthcare employees who had tried to raise the alarm over unsafe practices and were subsequently vilified (*Private Eye*, 2011). The idea of whistleblowing has gained respectability as a means to jolt industries into change and applying justice. The collapse of Enron in the United States and the expenses scandal among UK politicians have illustrated how unhealthy organizational practices can be exposed by one or two people. However, for most employees who have experienced the violation of their psychological contract with their workplace – perhaps because of a failed promotion, reduction in wages or pension rights, or job insecurity – the way to 'get even' is to adjust the job deal accordingly. Acts of organizational citizenship are among the first to suffer as people withdraw their commitment and, at the opposite extreme, sabotage can take many forms. Of course these are generally not condoned, especially where risky or unethical behavior ensues, but they tempt many who wish to make the job appear fairer to them. One study of 800 managers involved in ongoing organizational change found links between breaches in the psychological contract and subsequent poorer job performance, such as wasting time and dodging duties (Turnley and Feldman, 2000). Perhaps it is more accurate to suggest that taking something back from an employer who is perceived to have let you down is a form of channeling emotions. However, it is important to bear in mind the potential outcomes if things do get out of hand. Moving the manager's desk by one centimeter each day over six weeks so eventually the manager can no longer sit at it could be a cause for hilarity, unless as a result someone trips and falls, or the manager has no sense of humor! In terms of rewriting the psychological contract, the positive outcome is where levels of fairness, which may have been under attack, are increased (Rousseau and McLean Parks, 1993). This can be the most satisfying type of 'getting even' and, in the current economic climate, specific procedures for redress should be made clear or discovered afresh if none appear to exist. Knowing one's rights in employment law or consulting the relevant union or human resource department about organizational practices in times of flux, can prove helpful, reassuring the individual that at least in theory – and hopefully in practice – there is a means of recourse if the individual feels able to take it.

When it comes to rewriting the psychological contract for ourselves, we quickly gain a pretty good idea of what we can expect in terms of finances, expectations about working or not working for a period of time, as well as family dynamics in pressured circumstances. However, it is one thing to know this and another to manage how we and others feel about it. The following sections outline coping strategies which offer support via physical, emotional and behavioral channels in adjusting to unfamiliar and perhaps unwelcome realities.

De-stressing – physical strategies for more effective coping

Exercise

The popular conception is that we spend too little time undertaking the kind, or regularity, of physical activity which is beneficial for our health. Research findings appear to support this, with only 28 percent of working adults in the United Kingdom taking sufficient exercise (Cavill et al., 2006). The idea of rushing outside to think about a jog, some gentle lifting of weights or a visit to the local gym may bypass many, but the awareness of the potential consequences of the combination of stressful times and under-activity should encourage us to configure how we might do things at least a little differently for the good of our health. The link between psychological strain and physical well-being has been long recognized, and so elevated levels of blood pressure, increases in blood chemicals linked with poorer health (e.g., high-density lipoprotein cholesterol) and abdominal obesity are known responses to chronic exposure to stress at work.

The London-based study of 10,308 UK civil servants showed that, where individuals experience three or more incidences of strain due to the workplace, their chances of Metabolic Syndrome indicated by these physical symptoms are doubled (Chandola et al., 2006). In the recession of the early 1990s, European studies found increases in cholesterol among half of a sample of employees who were struggling with sleep difficulties at a time of threatened job loss (Mattiasson et al., 1990), and the risks of suffering coronary heart disease were predicted by factors such as job insecurity (Siegrist et al., 1990).

Such findings support the need for us to consider strategies which might benefit physical health, such as those discussed in other sections of this chapter, as well as positive changes to our levels of activity where necessary. Interventions sponsored by the workplace to improve physical health have been considered (see Chapter 5), but there is clearly a lot that the individual can do, whether working or not, provided this is considered safe by their medical advisor. A ten-year study of the male population of Caerphilly in South Wales found the risks to health – including cardiovascular disease – were lowered in line with increases in levels of physical activity. Furthermore, for middle-aged men with no previous history of coronary heart disease, intensive leisure-time physical activity, such as jogging, climbing stairs, swimming and heavy digging in the garden meant significantly reduced risks of mortality (Yu, Yarnell, Sweetnam and Murray, 2003). It is interesting that this study found no link between health risks and physical activity as part of one's job, which suggests that it is the formation of physically healthier habits in our whole lifestyles, not simply at work, which determines how we fare. The use of diaries to help plan and record physical activities, as well as having access to routes along which to walk, is known to aid improvements in healthy behavior (Dugdill et al., 2008) as these can help to strengthen the link between what we know we should do and what we achieve.

Taking time out

In challenging times, opportunities for relaxing or even the capability itself can desert us. The increased chances of worry clouding the mind mean that the quality of simple pleasures such as listening to music, taking a walk when the sun is shining, spending time with friends or watching a favorite television program can suffer. There are a number of relaxation methods which are designed both to reduce our physiological arousal when faced with stressors and to induce feelings of greater calm. This can have the psychological effect of dampening anxiety, providing a greater sense of control and also enhancing well-being. At a physical level, relaxation can keep blood pressure under control, reduce muscle tension, lower cholesterol in the bloodstream and improve clarity of thinking (Weinberg, Sutherland and Cooper, 2010). Learning and practicing a relaxation technique can allow the individual to use it at times of pressure to decrease the emotional impact of a stressor. Progressive muscle relaxation utilizes the alternate tensing and relaxation of muscle groups, for example, hands, shoulders, legs, and so forth, whereas meditation focuses the mind – often to the accompaniment of the repetition of one word – in order to clear one's thoughts. Biofeedback is a different technique which teaches the individual to control a particular aspect of functioning, such as heart rate, by using feedback – perhaps via an audible tone or a visual reading – to learn associations which maintain it at a particular level. Each of these techniques has been shown to produce positive benefits for well-being (Cooper and Cartwright, 1994; Squires, 2007).

With a similar outcome in mind, taking a break from a situation which is grinding us down, either by having a proper lunch hour or going out, reading or enjoying a pleasant view, can give us a chance to recharge our emotional batteries. Being able to 'switch off mentally', or psychologically detaching from a problem for a period of time, can help to lift an individual's mood and mean having more energy for leisure time at the end of a challenging day (Sonnentag and Bayer, 2005). This is not quite the same as avoiding one's problems altogether, but it can be part of shaping our habits to improve well-being when under pressure. At a physiological level, we are inundated with dietary advice to the point where we know what is probably good for us, but struggle to implement it! Simple guidance which incorporates a number of things we probably do, but are easily neglected, includes those strategies recommended in Table 6.2.

Setting the pace – emotional and behavioral coping techniques

Harnessing emotional intelligence

It has been the aim of this chapter to see how we might better deal with turbulent times by taking greater control over

Table 6.2   Small changes to enhance well-being while working

Recommendation	Benefit for well-being
Having breakfast	Improved cognitive performance later in the day
Reduce high caffeine intake from coffee and tea – drink water or juices instead	Less caffeine will mean reduced secretion of 'stress chemicals' into the bloodstream
Ensure appropriate intake of vitamins and minerals	Keeps levels maintained which otherwise can be depleted in times of pressure
Avoid excess fat intake	Reduces fat levels in the bloodstream which are already elevated when facing stressors
Plan and take breaks from your work in the evenings and at lunch-times	Improves psychological and physical recovery from demands of work
If working at home on any evenings, finish at least an hour before going to bed and do something which distracts you from work	Helps us to 'switch off' mentally and avoids that feeling of lying there feeling completely alert when we want to sleep!

Sources: Kanarek, 1997; Looker and Gregson, 1994; Sonnentag and Bayer, 2005.

those things which we are able to control. In considering how we might cope in terms of our emotions and behavior, it is an academic exercise to attempt to separate them and, so, they are addressed here together. In fact, one could reasonably argue that emotions and the way we respond to them pervade how we think and also how our bodies react. Perhaps it is fair to say that the impact of turbulent times is best measured in terms of the emotions experienced by those affected and the societies who seek change for the better as a result. As a crisis unfolds, most emotions are usually negative ; however, Chapter 1 of this book highlighted the presence of positive emotions which indicate the grittiness of our species in rising to such challenges. The economic collapse of the later years of the last decade was no different in that on the one hand it elicited outrage, alarm and bitter disappointment, and on the other acceptance, determination and courage. This, of course, is not just the prerogative of nations gripped by financial crisis, illustrated in national protests across a number of European countries, but also of those embroiled in political upheaval and even war.

Understandably, it is often the meaning of such events at an individual level which takes precedence. In recent years much has been written about the significance of our emotions, and written in a way which suggests that research into the subject has been ignored for far too long. One approach, which helps to provide insight into how we comprehend our own and others' emotions, is the concept of emotional intelligence (EI). This is the capacity to understand and harness, for largely positive purposes, emotions experienced by ourselves and others. Popularized by US psychologist and science journalist, Daniel Goleman, EI consists of four emotional and social competencies which form the basis for our communications and functioning in a range of settings, including work and personal relationships (Goleman, 2000):

- Self-awareness – the recognition of one's own emotions and their impact on others; the ability to identify and

appraise one's strengths and weaknesses; and possessing a sense of self-confidence
- Self-management – covers a range of abilities which enable us to keep control over our feelings, to build trust with others and to be conscientious and flexible while focusing on attaining our goals and demonstrating initiative.
- Social awareness – the capacity for sensing and gaining insight into the emotional circumstances of others, supporting them in their own development, identifying and meeting others' expectations and understanding the prevailing climate
- Relationship management – demonstrating successful social skills across settings which require sound two-way communication, persuasiveness, leadership, and the ability to handle conflict, promoting change and team-work

Although there is some disagreement about the extent to which these insights are reflections of our personalities and/or skills which can be learned, there is a growing body of evidence that points to the importance of EI for a range of positive outcomes (Ciarocchi, Forgas and Mayer, 2006). The relevance of EI is clearly elevated in turbulent times, as increased levels of expressed emotion – which we may witness on news broadcasts and in our own lives – tend to demand acknowledgement, comprehension and appropriate responses. Where emotions are accompanied by strong motivations to hang on to what we have become accustomed to, skills are required in managing expectations, whether these are hopes or fears. This is as true in our home lives as it is in the workplace (Lopes et al., 2005), and where high levels of EI are exhibited, this can be utilized to encourage positive communications with others (Sy et al., 2006). The impact of employees' EI on customers has been shown to have positive outcomes for customer perceptions and loyalty (Boxer and Rekettye, 2010), and there is no reason to suspect we behave so differently or fail to miss such opportunities in our relationships outside work.

It clearly makes sense to spend time and effort understanding others' viewpoints, especially in fast-moving circumstances. One factory manager whose job it was to announce redundancies and closures in a multinational company was sure that the reason he never encountered verbal abuse or worse, was his approach – carefully explaining the reasons for the situation, how the process would be managed and respectfully addressing all staff together. Organizations recognize the importance of such talents in change situations (Scott-Ladd and Chan, 2004), and one does not need to turn to recent publications to be aware of the sentiments expressed by best sellers such as Dale Carnegie's *How to Win Friends and Influence People*, or perhaps more fundamentally to see the principles of EI in action in any social situation we choose to examine. Each aspect of EI as described in Goleman's model is important. However, with turbulent times in mind, our level of success in managing emotions and relationships with those who matter to us, reflects the need for tolerance and patience. It is important to give ourselves time to realize why motivation is necessary, but why it is also harder to muster in dealing with crises. Being all things to all people is not always possible, and there may well be times when we feel burned out by the emotions we experience and by those we witness in others. This leads us to highlight the importance of nurturing positive emotions which will help to balance our emotional well-being.

Looking on the bright side

The importance of optimism has already been highlighted (see Chapter 2) and is perhaps an obvious component of effective emotional coping (Quick, Little and Nelson, 2009). However, it could itself be overoptimistic to expect anyone battling with adversity to develop a positive outlook if this is not their usual manner in appraising events. It is, therefore, an essential part of coping that we encourage hope in ourselves and others by having things to which we can look forward, by arranging social and other outlets for the expression of positive emotion.

This serves the purposes of encouraging engagement with others, providing a platform for mutual support, where this is appropriate, and giving those involved a break from focusing on trying circumstances. Gathering together is a natural part of human survival, and this is no less the case with psychological challenges. Part of the prospect of getting to the end of an emotional roller coaster ride is to know we are not alone on the journey. Whether it is meeting up with family, friends, colleagues or ex-colleagues, participating in or watching entertainment, sporting, religious or social events, the opportunities to get together are those which add to the emotional strength we need in turbulent times. Many positive psychological rewards are derived from such activity.

While positive relationships may not be easy in turbulent times, owing to the multifaceted stressors which are in evidence, we tend to be aware of what works for us. One study found that varying strategies appealed to occupational groups as diverse as teachers, nurses, mail-order supervisors and church ministers (Dewe and Guest, 1990). It was not clear from the findings how their use of coping mechanisms was determined by circumstance or choice, but social support and expressing emotions were more evident among the public sector employees compared to more passive approaches by the ministers. More recent research from the field of positive psychology has demonstrated the promise of a range of interventions designed to boost individuals' levels of happiness, whether from a high or low starting point (Seligman, Steen, Park and Peterson, 2005).

Case study 6.1 Coping and comedy

A show promoting mental health, called 'Cracking Up', the creation of London-based comedian and former social services' housing officer, John Ryan, illustrates the significance of what it is that leads us to a breaking point and, hopefully, away again. Ryan's show, which debuted at the Soho Theatre in London, is performed to a variety of audiences, ranging from men's health groups to the armed services, and staged in locations as varied as sports grounds to military bases. Among the many notable things about Ryan is his interpersonal style which is no different offstage as on, as well as his recognition that the serious issue of psychological health is often underplayed, and that it benefits from the comic perspective. There is an assertion that creativity is spurred on by emotional challenge and, arguably, there is none greater than doing stand-up comedy to a platoon of servicemen and women still reeling from their tour of duty. The artistic producer, Jonathon Miller, points out that for audiences enduring hard times there is the sense of companionship derived from a common experience which mirrors their daily existence, while the playwright, Steven Berkoff, emphasizes the 'spiritual sustenance' which live performance can offer, 'where one does not feel cheated, because what you see is what you get'. Their comments resonate with turbulent times and, in our own way, we all find that coping is a creative process which thrives on unusual circumstances. This has often been demonstrated in times of national and international crisis, which have produced advances in scientific discovery as well as providing the spur for great literature, art and music.

Challenging and coaching our own behavior

Regulating our emotions and behavior so that these do not jeopardize the outcomes we desire in difficult employment situations and in life outside work is not always easy. The desired approach is somewhere between emotion-focused and problem-focused coping (Lazarus and Folkman, 1984), in which the following steps may feature:

- Acknowledge the existence of a problem
- Identify the relevant parties who are affected by it
- Communicate effectively with all concerned
- Adjust expectations accordingly
- Generate potential solutions
- Negotiate for new reasonable terms where old ones are no longer applicable. (see Weinberg and Cooper, 2007)

It is commonly assumed that all individuals – inside and outside work – are familiar with the skills necessary to see this process through, but often these skills are only acquired via experience. Without these skills, problems can escalate, communication can suffer and it might be too late to prevent recurrence of the problem. As the assumption is that people 'should' have the appropriate skills to deal with challenging situations to some degree of competence, the role of training (at work) or learning from others (outside work) is frequently underestimated. If we are immersed in a problematic situation from which it becomes difficult to step away, the hamster-wheel scenario persists and we can continue to behave (and deal with emotions) in the same manner as before. This applies to situations in all aspects of life. However, those skills for which workplaces may be more inclined to prepare us are assertiveness, time management and conflict management. It is galling that these essential life skills receive little attention in our preparations for adult life, and we may find that in close relationships, the opportunities to 'see what works' may well be limited. At least by creating, or taking, opportunities to learn, we stand to gain from getting things right at some point. In relation to job-hunting, we learn the value of preparation for interviews, practicing answers, imagining ourselves in the shoes of our prospective employers and being able to reinvent ourselves for each opportunity that comes our way. It is obviously not quite the same when it comes to personal relationships, although it could be argued that there are elements in common. As long as we can accept that mistakes are part of the human condition, then we will feel more inclined to bounce back as necessary.

Throughout the process of coping with problem situations and difficult times, we may find we are coaching ourselves to do better and to face the next challenge. Family and friends can be major sources of support, but these may not always be accessible. Either way, our personal 'training' from learning and past experience, and the psychological resources we carry with us, are among our greatest assets. If the turbulence in our lives is related to being out of work, then we tend to value the importance of maintaining a routine and occupying ourselves with productive tasks – from voluntary work to acquiring new skills and job-seeking – so that we are psychologically prepared to return to work. If we are facing uncertain or challenging situations inside or outside work, then seeking support and advice is particularly helpful, as otherwise we can feel alone in having to deal with such circumstances. In addition, at some level we may find we can exert limited control over at least one aspect of our lives, so that there is a source of positive feedback which, in turn, is important for our self-belief and self-esteem. Even if we have doubts about our resilience in turbulent times, we need to recognize there are core parts of our psyche which are designed to adapt. Our mission – which as a species we have chosen to accept over tens of thousands of years – is to recognize our potential psychological strengths and deploy them to meet the challenge at hand.

Alexander Consulting Group (1989) *Employee Assistance Program Financial Offset Study*. Westport, CT: Alexander and Alexander.

Andersen, L.B. (2004) 'Relative risk of mortality in the physically inactive is underestimated because of real changes in exposure level during follow-up', *American Journal of Epidemiology* 160, 189–95.

Aronson, E. (1984) *The Social Animal*, 4th edn. New York: W.H. Freeman and Company.

Arthur, A.R. (2002) 'Mental health problems and British workers: A survey of mental health problems in employees who receive counseling from Employee Assistance Programmes', *Stress and Health* 18, 69–74.

Arthur, A.R. (2000) 'Employee assistance programmes: The emperor's new clothes of stress management', *British Journal of Guidance and Counselling* 28, 549–59.

Aust, B. and Ducki, A. (2004) 'Comprehensive health promotion interventions at the workplace: Experiences with health circles in Germany', *Journal of Occupational Health Psychology* 9, 258–70.

BACP (2009) 'Guidelines for Counselling in the Workplace: A Free Resource for Employers'. Available at http://www.bacp.co.uk/admin/structure/files/pdf/3805_acw_guidelines_web.pdf.

Baron, K.G., Smith, T.W., Butner, J., Nealey-Moore, J., Hawkins, M.W. and Uchino, B.N. (2007) 'Hostility, anger and marital adjustment: Concurrent and prospective associations with psychosocial vulnerability', *Journal of Behavioural Medicine* 30, 1–10.

BBC News (2011) 'Bank bonuses to run to billions in 2011', 7 January. Available at http://www.bbc.co.uk/news/business-12131092, accessed on 22 July 2011.

BBC News (2010) 'Bank bonus limit agreed by European Parliament'. Available at http://www.bbc.co.uk/news/10534195, accessed on 20 July 2011.

Benson, H. (1993) 'The relaxation response', in D. Goldman and J. Gurin (eds) *Mind/Body Medicine*. New York: Consumer Reports Books.

Benson, H. (1976) *The Relaxation Response*. New York: Morrow.

Berlin, J.A. and Colditz, G.A. (1990) 'A meta-analysis of physical activity in the prevention of coronary heart disease', *American Journal of Epidemiology* 132 (4), 612–28.

Black Report (2008) 'Working for a healthier tomorrow'. Available at www.workingforhealth.gov.uk/documents/working-for-a-healthier-tomorrow-tagged.pdf, accessed on 19 November 2009.

Blackman, M. (2008) 'The effective interview', in S. Cartwright and C.L. Cooper (eds) *Oxford Handbook of Personnel Psychology*. Oxford: Oxford University Press, 194–214.

Bond, F.W. and Bunce, D. (2000) 'Mediators of change in emotion-focused and problem-focused worksite stress management interventions', *Journal of Occupational Health Psychology* 5, 156–63.

Bordia, P., Restubog, S., Lloyd, D. and Tang, R.L. (2008) 'When employees strike back: Investigating mediating mechanisms between psychological contract breach and workplace deviance', *Journal of Applied Psychology* 93, 1104–17.

Borrill, C.S., Wall, T.D., West, M.A., Hardy, G.E., Shapiro, D.A., Haynes, C.E., Stride, C.B., Woods, D. and Carter, A.J. (1998) *Stress among Staff in NHS Trusts: Final Report*, Institute of Work Psychology, University of Sheffield and Psychological Therapies Research Centre, University of Leeds.

Boxer, I. and Rekettye, G. (2010) 'The influence of perceived emotional intelligence on perceived service value and customer loyalty', *Acta Oeconomica* 60 (3), 255–73.

Bradon, P. (2009) 'The Best Companies to Work For'. Available at http//business.timesonline.co.uk/tol/business/career_and_jobs/article6850595.ece, accessed on 26 February 2010.

Brough, P. and O'Driscoll, M. (2005) 'Work-family conflict and stress', in A-S. Antoniou and C.L. Cooper (eds) *Research Companion to Organizational Health Psychology*. Cheltenham: Edward Elgar, 346–65.

Brown, G.W. and Harris, T. (1978) *Social Origins of Depression – A Study of Psychiatric Disorder in Women*. London: Routledge.

Bull, F.C., Adams, E.J., Hooper, P.L. and Jones, C.A. (2008) *Well@ Work: A Summary Report and Calls to Action*. London: British Heart Foundation.

Burcell, B. (2011) 'A temporal comparison of the effects of unemployment and job insecurity on well-being', Sociological Research online, http://www.socresonline.org.uk/16/1/9.html, accessed on 22 July 2011.

Carroll, M. (1996) *Workplace Counselling*. London: Sage.

Carver, C.S. and Connor-Smith, J. (2010) 'Personality and coping'. *Annual Review of Psychology* 61, 679–704.

Cavill, N., Kahlmeier, S. and Racioppi, F. (2006) 'Physical Activity and Health in Europe: Evidence for Action', WHO Europe, Copenhagen.

CCH (2007) 'Unscheduled Absence Survey'. Available at http://hr.cch.com/press/releases/20071010h.asp, accessed on 30 November 2009.

Chandola, T., Britton, A., Brunner, E., Hemingway, H., Malik, M., Kumari, M., Badrick, E., Kivimaki, M. and Marmot, M.G. (2008) 'Work stress and coronary heart disease: What are the mechanisms?', *European Heart Journal* 29, 640–48.

Chandola, T., Brunner, E. and Marmot, M. (2006) 'Chronic stress at work and the metabolic syndrome: Prospective study', *BMJ (Clinical Research Ed.)* 332, 521–25.

Chang, K. and Lu, L. (2007) 'Characteristics of organizational culture, stressors and well-being – The case of Taiwanese organizations', *Journal of Managerial Psychology* 22 (6), 549–68.

Ciarocchi, J., Forgas, J. and Mayer, J. (2006) *Emotional Intelligence in Everyday Life: A Scientific Enquiry.* New York: Psychology Press.

CIPD (2009) 'Employee engagement'. Available at http://www.cipd. co.uk/subjects/empreltns/general/empengmt.htm, accessed on 9 November 2010.

CIPD (2006) 'Working Life: Employee Attitudes and Engagement'. Available at http://www.cipd.co.uk/publicpolicy/_mntlcptl.htm, accessed on December 2006.

Clare, A. (1980) *Psychiatry in Dissent*, 2nd edn. London: Tavistock.

Clark, A. (2010a) 'Classic case of two worlds colliding'. *The Guardian*, 7 October.

Clark, A. (2010b) 'Economists say White House bailouts saved 8.5m US jobs'. *The Guardian*, 29 July.

Clark, A. (2009) 'Crisis Management'. *The Guardian*, 21 October.

Clow, A. (2001) 'The physiology of stress', in F. Jones and J. Bright (eds) *Stress: Myth, Theory and Research.* Harlow: Pearson Education Limited.

Confederation of British Industry, CBI/AXA (2007) *Attending to Absence: Absence and Labour Turnover Survey 2007.* London: Confederation of British Industry.

Confederation of British Industry, CBI/AXA (2006) 'Cost of UK workplace absence tops £13bn – New CBI survey'. Available at http//:www. cbi.org.uk/ndbs/press.nsf, accessed on 15 May 2011.

Cooper, C.L., Bebbington, P.E., Meltzer, H., Bhugra, D., Brugha, T., Jenkins, R., Farrell, M. and King, M. (2008) 'Depression and common mental disorders in lone parents: Results of the 2000 National Psychiatric Morbidity Survey', *Psychological Medicine* 38, 335–42.

Cooper, C.L. and Bramwell, R. (1992) 'A comparative analysis of occupational stress in managerial and shopfloor workers in the brewing industry: Mental health, job satisfaction and sickness', *Work and Stress* 6, 127–38.

Cooper, C.L. and Cartwright, S. (1994) 'Healthy mind; healthy organization – A proactive approach to occupational stress', *Human Relations* 47, 455–71.

Cooper, C.L. and Dewe, P. (2008) 'Well-being – absenteeism, presenteeism, costs and challenges', *Occupational Medicine* 58 (8), 522–24.

Cooper, C.L. and Dewe, P. (2004) *Stress: A Brief History.* Oxford: Blackwell.

Cooper, C.L. and Sutherland, V.J. (1992) 'Job stress, satisfaction, and mental health among general practitioners before and after introduction of new contract', *British Medical Journal* 304, 1545–48.

Cooper, C.L., Sloan, S. and Williams, S. (1988) *The Occupational Stress Indicator*. Berkshire: NFER-Nelson.

Costa, P.T., Jr and McCrae, R.R. (1992) *NEO-PIR Professional Manual*. Odessa, FL: Psychological Assessment Resources.

Cvengros, J.A., Christensen, A.J. and Lawton, W.J. (2005) 'Health locus of control and depression in chronic kidney disease: A dynamic perspective', *Journal of Health Psychology* 10, 677–87.

David, D., Montgomery, G.H. and Bovbjerg, D.H. (2006) 'Relations between coping responses and optimism-pessimism in predicting anticipatory psychological distress in surgical breast cancer patients', *Personality and Individual Differences* 40 (2), 203–13.

Dewe, P.J. and Guest, D.E. (1990) 'Methods of coping with stress at work: A conceptual analysis and empirical study of measurement issues', *Journal of Organisational Behaviour* 11, 135–50.

Dewe, P.J., O'Driscoll, M. and Cooper, S.L. (2010) *Coping with Work Stress*. Oxford: Wiley-Blackwell.

DHSSPS (2004) 'Stress, mental health and suicide: Employment status'. http://docs.google.com/viewer?a=v&q=cache:rvawBCt67UwJ: www.dhsspsni.gov.uk/mentalhealthunemployment.pdf+dhsspsni. govunemployment&hl=en&gl=uk&pid=bl&srcid=ADGEESi3 W2-QHaa4WvbwTcWzb0JSjZuKAtAsRJ7S_v_oR6UnjITdoD- km5ij0OzlgCjzlwAvMULhzP4aDJpKGaIh4mvB9NiHF9rl- CaiuZ5c555ghQAsV6_glvtkwrPWuBphmh6MlZU52T&sig=AHIE tbR3epEpQLcvlhW-Rtc5QZew_Crqnw. Available at dhsspsni.gov, accessed on 3 June 2011.

Dishman, R.D. (1988) *Exercise Adherence: Its Impact on Public Health*. Champaign, IL: Human Kinetics Books.

Dugdill, L., Brettle, A., Hulme, C., McCluskey, S. and Long, A.F. (2008) 'Workplace physical activity interventions: A systematic review', *International Journal of Workplace Health Management* 1 (1), 20–40.

Eaves v Blaenclydach Colliery (1909) 2 K.B. (Eng.) 73.

Eaves v Blaenclydach Colliery Company Ltd (1909) in J. Earnshaw and C.L. Cooper, *Work and Stress*, 8, 287–95.

Ebstrup, J.F., Eplov, L.F., Pisinger, C. and Jorgensen, T. (2011) 'Association between the five factor personality traits and perceived stress: Is the effect mediated by general self-efficacy?', *Anxiety, Stress, Coping* 24 (4), 407–19.

Edmans, A. (2008) 'Does the stock market fully value intangibles? Employee satisfaction and equity prices', SSRN (Social Science Research Network): http://ssrn.com/abstract = 985735.

Elkin, A.J. and Rosch, P.J. (1990) 'Promoting mental health at the workplace: The prevention side of stress management', *Occupational Medicine: State of the Art Review* 5 (4), 739–54.

Ellis, A. (1977) 'The basic clinical theory of rational-emotive therapy', in A. Ellis and R. Grieger (eds) *Handbook of Rational-Emotive Therapy*. New York: Springer-Verlag.

Erfurt, J.C., Foote, A. and Heirich, M.A. (1992) 'The cost-effectiveness of worksite wellness programs for hypertension control, weight loss, smoking cessation and exercise', *Personnel Psychology* 45, 5–27.

Eurofound (2010) 'European Working Conditions Survey Results, 2010'. Available at http://www.eurofound.europa.eu/surveys/smt/ewcs/ewcs2010_07_06.htm, accessed on 15 July 2011.

Ewers, P., Bradshaw, T., McGovern, J., Ewers, B., Ewers, P., Bradshaw, T., McGovern, J. and Ewers, B. (2002) 'Does training in psychosocial interventions reduce burnout rates in forensic nurses?', *Journal of Advanced Nursing* 37, 470–76.

Federal Bureau of Investigation (2009) Available at http://www2.fbi.gov/ucr/cius2009/index.html, accessed on 20 July 2011.

Ferrie, J.E., Shipley, M.J., Stansfeld, S.A. and Marmot, M. (2002) 'Effects of job insecurity and change in job security on self-reported health, psychiatric morbidity, physiological measure and health-related behaviours in British civil servants: The Whitehall study', *Journal of Epidemiology and Community Health* 56, 450–54.

Fitch, C., Hamilton, S., Basset, P. and Davey, R. (2009) *Debt and Mental Health*. London: Royal College of Psychiatrists.

Foresight Project (2008) 'Mental Capital and Wellbeing'. Available at www.foresight.gov.uk/Ourwork/ActiveProjects/Mental%20Capital/Welcome.asp

Freedy, J.R. and Hobfoll, S.E. (1994) 'Stress inoculation for reduction of burnout: A conservation of resources approach', *Anxiety, Stress and Coping* 6, 311–25.

French, J.R.P., Jr, Caplan, R.D. and Harrison, R. (1982) *The Mechanisms of Job Stress and Strain*. Chichester: John Wiley and Sons.

Friedman, M. and Rosenman, R.H. (1974) *Type A Behaviour and Your Heart*. New York: Knopf.

Giga, S.I. and Cooper, C.L. (2003) 'Psychological contracts within the NHS', *Human Givens Journal* 10, 38–40.

Giga, S.I., Cooper, C.L. and Faragher, B. (2003) 'The development of a framework for a comprehensive approach to stress management interventions at work', *International Journal of Stress Management* 10, 280–96.

Gilbreath, B. and Benson, P.G. (2004) 'The contribution of supervisor behaviour to employee psychological well-being', *Work and Stress* 18, 255–67.

Glozier, N., Hough, C., Henderson, M. and Holland-Elliott, K. (2006) 'Attitudes of nursing staff towards co-workers returning from psychiatric and physical illnesses', *International Journal of Social Psychiatry* 52, 525–34.

Goetzel, R., Long, S., Ozminkowski, R., Hawkins, K., Wang, S. and Lynch, W. (2004) 'Health, absence, disability and presenteeism cost estimates of certain physical and mental health conditions affecting U.S. employers', *Journal of Occupational and Environmental Medicine* 46, 398–412.

Goleman, D. (2000) 'Intelligent leadership', *Executive Excellence* 3, 17.

Grawitch, M.J., Trares, S. and Kohler, J.M. (2007) 'Healthy workplace practices and employee health', *International Journal of Stress Management* 14 (3), 275–93.

Greenberg, J. (1987) 'A taxonomy of organizational justice theories'. *Academy of Management Review* 12, 9–22.

Guardian (2011a) 'City bonus row is reignited after £14bn is paid out'. Available at http://www.guardian.co.uk/business/2011/jul/19/bonuses-executive-pay-banks, accessed on 20 July 2011.

Guardian (2011b) 'More than 3m households in financial difficulty', 13 July.

Guardian (2011c) 'Job losses cost UK employers £13.4bn over three years', 4 July.

Guardian (2011d) 'Relegation, riots – now River Plate fans confront reality', 28 June.

Guardian (2011e) 'Poor GDP figures add to pressure on Osborne', 28 June.

Guardian (2011f) 'Rising petrol prices will causes drivers to reduce family trips', 22 June.

Guardian (2011g) 'Irish people "complicit in banking collapse"', 20 April.

Guardian (2011h) 'Fox apologises for army emails sacking soldiers', 15 February.

Guardian (2010a) 'Osborne sees the road to recovery as opposition warns of "reckless gamble"', 30 November.

Guardian (2010b) 'Recession causes surge in mental health problems'. Available at http://www.guardian.co.uk/society/2010/apr/01/recession-surge-mental-health-problems, accessed on 22 July 2011.

Guardian (2005) 'Suicide blights China's young adults', 26 July.

Guthrie, E. (2008) 'Medically unexplained symptoms in primary care', *Advances in Psychiatric Treatment* 14, 432–40.

Health Education Authority (1997) *Organizational Stress: Planning and Implementing a Programme to Address Organizational Stress in the NHS.* London: HEA.

Herriot, P. and Pemberton, C. (1995) *New Deals.* Chichester: John Wiley and Sons.

Hilton, M.F., Sheridan, J., Cleary, C.M. and Whiteford, H.A. (2009) 'Employee absenteeism measures reflecting current work practices may be instrumental in a re-evaluation of the relationship between psychological distress/mental health and absenteeism', *International Journal of Methods in Psychiatric Research* 18 (1), 37–47.

Hobsbawm, E. (1994) *The Age of Extremes: The Short Twentieth Century 1914–1991*. London: Abacus.

Hoel, H., Cooper, C.L. and Faragher, B. (2001) 'The experience of bullying in the UK: The impact of organizational status', *European Journal of Work and Organizational Psychology* 10, 443–65.

Hoel, H., Faragher, B. and Cooper, C.L. (2004) 'Bullying is detrimental to health, but all bullying behaviours are not necessarily equally damaging', *British Journal of Guidance and Counselling* 32, 367–87.

Houtman, I. (2005) 'Costs related to work-related stress'. Available at http://www.eurofound.europa.eu/ewco/reports/TN0502TR01/TN0502TR01_7.htm, accessed on 6 July 2011.

Home Office/ONS (2011) Available at http://www.homeoffice.gov.uk/publications/science-research-statistics/research-statistics/crime-research/hosb1011/hosb1011snr?view=Binary, accessed on 20 July 2011.

HSE (2009) 'Stress-related and psychological disorders: Summary'. Available at www.hse.gov.uk/statistics/causdis/stress/index.htm, accessed on 12 February 2010

Huxley, P., Evans, S., Gately, C., Webber, M., Mears, A., Pajak, S., Kendall, T., Medina, J. and Katona, C. (2005) 'Stress and pressures in mental health social work: The worker speaks', *British Journal of Social Work* 35, 1063–79.

Industrial Society (2001) *Flexible Work Patterns*. Managing Best Practice, no. 85. London: Industrial Society.

Jacobson, E. (1938) *Progressive Relaxation*. Chicago: University of Chicago Press.

James, O. (2007) *Affluenza*. London: Vermillion.

Jenkins, P. (2010) 'Stress and the Law', in A. Weinberg, V.J. Sutherland and C.L. Cooper (eds) *Organizational Stress Management: A Strategic Approach*. Basingstoke: Palgrave Macmillan, 37–52.

Kagan, N. I., Kagan H. and Watson, M.G. (1995) 'Stress reduction in the workplace: The effectiveness of psychoeducational programs', *Journal of Counseling Psychology* 42 (1), 71–8.

Kanarek, R. (1997) 'Psychological effects of snacks and altered meal frequency', *British Journal of Nutrition* Supplement 1, 105–20.

Karasek, R. (1990) 'Lower health risk with increased job control among white collar workers', *Journal of Organizational Behavior* 11 (3), 171–85.

Kauffeld, S., Jonas, E. and Frey, D. (2004) 'Effects of a flexible work-time design on employee and company-related aims', *European Journal of Work and Organizational Psychology* 13, 17–100.

Keane, A., Ducette, J. and Adler, D.C. (1985) 'Stress in ICU and non-ICU nurses', *Nursing Research* 34, 231–36.

Kerr, J.H. and Vos, M.C.H. (1993) 'Employee fitness and general well-being', *Work and Stress* 7 (2), 179–90.

Kessler, R.C. and Frank, R.G. (1997) 'The impact of psychiatric disorders on work loss days', *Psychological Medicine* 27, 179–90.

Kessler, R.C., Greenberg, P.E., Mickelson, K.D., Meneades, L.M. and Wang, P.S. (2001) 'The effects of chronic medical conditions on work loss and work cutback', *Journal of Occupational and Environmental Medicine* 43 (3) 218–25.

Kinman, G. and Jones, F. (2004) *Working to the Limit*. London: AUT.

Kinnunen, U., Mauno, S., Geurts, S. and Dikkers, J. (2005) 'Work-family culture: Theoretical and empirical approaches', in S. Poelmans (ed.) *Work and Family: An International Research Perspective*. Mahwah, NJ: Lawrence Erlbaum Associates, 87–120.

Knechtle, B. (2004) 'Influence of physical activity on mental well-being and psychiatric disorders', *Praxis* 93 (35), 1403–11.

Kobasa, S. (1979) 'Stressful life events, personality and health: An enquiry into hardiness', *Journal of Personality and Social Psychology* 37 (1), 1–11.

Laszlo, K.D., Pikhart, H., Kopp, M.S., Bobak, M., Pajak, K., Malyutina, S., Salavecz, G. and Marmot, M. (2010) 'Job insecurity and health: A study of 16 European countries' *Social Science Medicine*, March; 70(6–3): 867–874.

Lazarus, R. (1993) 'Coping theory and research: Past, present and future', *Psychosomatic Medicine* 55, 234–47.

Lazarus, R. and Folkman, S. (1984) *Stress, Appraisal and Coping*. New York: Springer Publications.

Leach, D.J., Jackson, P.R. and Wall, T.D. (2001) 'Realising the potential of empowerment: The impact of a feedback intervention on the performance of a complex technology', *Ergonomics* 44, 870–86.

Lee, C. and Gray, J.A. (1994) 'The role of employee assistance programmes', in C.L. Cooper and S. Williams (eds) *Creating Healthy Work Organizations*. Chichester: John Wiley and Sons, 214–41.

Leka, S., Griffiths, A. and Cox, T. (2007) 'Work, organisation and stress', in *Protecting Workers' Health Series*, no. 3. Nottingham: Institute of Work, Health and Organisations.

Leopold, J. (ed.) (2002) *Human Resources in Organizations*. Harlow: Prentice Hall.

Lerner, Y., Kertes, J. and Zilber, N. (2005) 'Immigrants from the former Soviet Union, 5 years post-immigration to Israel: Adaptation and risks factors for psychological distress'. *Journal of Psychological Medicine* 35, 1805–14.

Littlewood, S., Case, R., Gater, R. and Lindsey, C. (2003) 'Recruitment, retention, satisfaction and stress in child and adolescent psychiatrists', *Psychiatric Bulletin* 27, 61–7.

Looker, O. and Gregson, T. (1994) 'The biological basis of stress management', *British Journal of Guidance and Counselling* 22, 13–26.

Lopes, P.N., Salovey, P., Côté, S. and Beers, M. (2005) 'Emotion regulation abilities and the quality of social interaction'. *Emotion* 5 (1), 113–18.

Maltby, J., Day, L. and Macaskill, A. (2010) *Personality, Individual Differences and Intelligence*, 2nd edn. Harlow: Prentice Hall.

MacDermott, D. (2010) 'Psychological hardiness and meaning making as protection against sequelae in veterans of the wars in Iraq and Afghanistan'. *International Journal of Emergency Mental Health* 12 (3), 199–206.

Marchington, M., Grimshaw, D., Rubery, J. and Willmott, H. (2005) *Fragmenting Work: Blurring Organizational Boundaries and Disordering Hierarchies*. Oxford: Oxford University Press.

Martinez, J.C. (1994) 'Perceived control and feedback in judgement and memory', *Journal of Research in Personality* 28, 374–81.

Maruta, T., Colligan, R.C., Malinchoc, M. and Offord, K.P. (2000) 'Optimists v pessimists: Survival rate among medical patients over a 30 year period', *Mayo Clinic Proceedings* 75, 140–43.

Masi, D.A. and Jacobson, J.M. (2003) 'Outcome measurements of an integrated employee assistance and work-life program', *Research on Social Work Practice* 13, 451–67.

Maslach, C. and Jackson, S. (1986) *The Maslach Burnout Inventory*. Palo Alto: Consulting Psychologists Press.

Mattiasson, I., Lindärde, R., Hilsson, J.A. and Theorell, T. (1990) 'Threat of unemployment and cardiovascular risk factors: Longitudinal study of quality of sleep and serum cholesterol concentrations in men threatened with redundancy', *British Medical Journal* 310, 461–66.

Mayer, J.D., Caruso, D. and Salovey, P. (1999) 'Emotional intelligence meets traditional standards for an intelligence', *Intelligence* 27, 267–98.

McKinsey (2011) 'The growing US jobs challenge', *McKinsey Quarterly*, June. Available at http://www.mckinseyquarterly.com/The_growing_ US_jobs_challenge_2816, accessed on 31 July 2011.

McLeod, J. (2008) *Counselling in the Workplace: A Comprehensive Review of the Research Evidence,* 2nd edn. Lutterworth: BACP.

McLeod, J. (2001) *Counselling in the Workplace: The Facts. A Systematic Study of the Research Evidence*. Warwickshire: British Association for Counselling and Psychotherapy.

McLeod, J. and Henderson, M. (2003) 'Does workplace counselling work?' *British Journal of Psychiatry* 182, 103–4.

McManus, S., Meltzer, H., Brugha, T., Bebbington, P. and Jenkins, R. (2009) *Adult Psychiatric Morbidity in England, 2007: Results of a Household Survey*. Leeds: NHS Information Centre.

Meichenbaum, D. (1977) *Cognitive-Behaviour Modification*. New York: Plenum Press.

Mental Health Foundation (2011) 'Mental health statistics: The most common mental health problems'. Available at http://www.mental-health.org.uk/help-information/mental-health-statistics/common-mental-health-problems/, accessed on 6 July 2011.

Michie, S. and Sandhu, S. (1994) 'Stress management for clinical medical students', *Medical Education* 28, 528–33.

Mohanty, M. (2009) 'Effects of happiness on positive attitudes and wage: Evidence from the US data'. *Journal of Economic Psychology* 30 (6), 884–97.

Morgan, S.J. (2011) 'Are you being outsourced?' *The Psychologist* 24 (3), 182–85.

Murphy, L.R. (1996) 'Stress management techniques: Secondary prevention of stress', in M.J. Schabracq, J.A.M. Winnubst and C.L. Cooper (eds) *Handbook of Work and Health Psychology*. Chichester: John Wiley and Sons, 427–41.

Nadaoka, T., Kashiwakura, M., Oija, A., Morioka, Y. and Totsuka, S (1997) 'Stress and psychiatric disorders in local government officials in Japan, in relation to their employment level', *Acta Psychiatrica Scandinavica* 96, 176–83.

Ndlovu, N. and Parumasur, S.B. (2005) 'The perceived impact of downsizing and organizational transformation on survivors'. *South African Journal of Industrial Psychology* 31 (2), 14–21.

Netterstrom, B. and Juel, K. (1988) 'Impact of work-related and psychosocial factors on the development of ischaemic heart disease among urban bus drivers in Denmark', *Scandinavian Journal of Work and Environmental Health* 14, 231–38.

NICE – National Institute for Clinical Excellence (2009) *Public Health Guidance 22, Promoting Mental Wellbeing through Productive and Healthy Working Conditions: Guidance for Employers*. London: NICE.

Nicot, A-M. (2010) 'Female workers more prone to psychological disorders'. Available at http://www.eurofound.europa.eu/ewco/2009/04/FR0904049I.htm, accessed on 10 July 2011.

O'Driscoll, M.P., Poelmans, S., Spector, P.E., Kalliath, T., Allen, T.D., Cooper, C.L. and Sanchez, J.I. (2003) 'Family-responsive interventions, perceived organizational and supervisor support, work-family conflict, and psychological strain', *International Journal of Stress Management* 10, 326–44.

Office for National Statistics (2001) *Psychiatric morbidity among adults living in private households, 2000*. London: TSO.

Office of Population Census and Surveys (2002) *British Household Psychiatric Survey*. London: HMSO.

Office of Population Census and Surveys (1995) *British Household Psychiatric Survey*. London: HMSO.

Osborne, H. (2009) 'Part-time UK workers agree to cut hours to avoid the sack: What if it happens to you? Key points'. *The Guardian*, 13 March.

Palmer, S. (1997) 'Self acceptance: Concept, techniques and interventions'. *The Rational Emotive Behaviour Therapist* 5 (1), 4–30.

Palmer, S. and Cooper, C.L. (2010) *How to Deal with Stress*. London: Kogan Page.

Parks, T. (2009) *The Prince by Niccolo Machiavelli*. London: Penguin.

Personnel Today (2008) 'Job cuts hit older workers as unemployment levels reach 10-year high', 22 September.

Private Eye (2011) 'Whistleblowing Special Edition', 1292, 8 July.

Powell, L. (1992) 'The cognitive underpinnings of coronary-prone behaviours', *Cognitive Therapy and Research* 16, 123–42.

Quick, J., Little, L. and Nelson, D. (2009). 'Positive emotions, attitudes and health: Motivated, engaged, focussed', in S. Cartwright and C.L. Cooper (eds) *Oxford Handbook of Organizational Wellbeing*. Oxford: Oxford University Press, 214–35.

Randall, R., Griffiths, A. and Cox, T. (2005) 'Evaluating organizational stress-management interventions using adapted study designs', *European Journal of Work and Organizational Psychology* 14, 23–41.

Rhoades, L. and Eisenberger, R. (2002) 'Perceived organizational support: A review of the literature', *Journal of Applied Psychology* 87, 698–714.

Robinson, D., Perryman, S. and Hayday, S. (2004) 'The drivers of employee engagement', *IES Report*: London.

Rosenman, R., Friedman, M., Straus, R., Wurm, M., Kositchek, R., Hahn, W. and Werthessen, N. (1964) 'A predictive study of coronary heart disease', *Journal of the American Medical Association* 232, 872–77.

Rotter, J.B. (1966) 'Generalized expectancies for internal versus external control of reinforcement', *Psychological Monographs* 91, 482–97.

Rousseau, D. and McLean Parks, J. (1993) 'The contracts of individuals and organizations,' in B.M. Staw (ed.) *Research in Organizational Behavior* vol. 15. CA: JAI Press, 1–43.

Royal College of Psychiatrists (1995) *Defeat Depression Campaign*. London: Royal College of Psychiatrists.

Sainsbury Centre for Mental Health (2007) 'Mental health at work: Developing the business case'. Policy Paper 8. London: Sainsbury Centre for Mental Health.

Sanderman, R. (1998) 'New insights into the onset of heart disease and cancer', paper given at the 22nd European Conference on Psychosomatic Research, University of Manchester.

Saurel-Cubizolles, M.J., Zeitlin, J., Lelong, N., Papiernik, E., Di Renzo, G.C. and Breart, G. (2004) 'Employment, working conditions, and pre-term birth: Results from the Europop case-control survey', *Journal of Epidemiology and Community Health* 58, 395–401.

Schou, I., Ekeberg, O. and Ruland, C.M. (2005) 'The mediating role of appraisal and coping in the relationship between optimism-pessimism and quality of life', *Psycho-oncology* 14, 718–27.

Scott, H. (2002) 'Nursing profession is finding it harder to retain nurses', *British Journal of Nursing* 11, 1052.

Scott-Ladd, B. and Chan, C.A. (2004) 'Emotional intelligence and participation in decision making: Strategies for promoting organizational learning and change', *Strategic Change* 13, 95–105.

Selye, H. (1956) *The Stress of Life.* New York: McGraw-Hill.

Seymour, L. and Grove, B. (2005) *Work Interventions for People with Common Mental Health Problems.* London: British Occupational Health Research Foundation.

Shigemi, J., Mino, Y., Ohtsu, T. and Tsuda, T. (2000) 'Effects of perceived job stress on mental health: A longitudinal survey in a Japanese electronics company', *European Journal of Epidemiology* 16, 371–76.

Siegrist, J. (2009) 'Job control and reward: Effects on wellbeing', in S. Cartwright and C.L. Cooper (eds) *Oxford Handbook of Organizational Wellbeing.* Oxford: Oxford University Press, 109–32.

Siegrist, J., Peter, R., Junge, A., Cremer, P. and Seidel, D. (1990) 'Low status control, high effort at work and ischaemic heart disease: Prospective evidence from blue collar men', *Social Science and Medicine* 31, 1127–34.

Silvester, J. and Anderson, N. (2003) 'Technology and discourse: A comparison of face-to-face and telephone employment interviews', *International Journal of Selection and Assessment* 11, 206–14.

Skapinakis, P., Welch, S., Lewis, G., Singleton, N. and Araya, R. (2006) 'Socio-economic position and common mental disorders: Longitudinal study in the general population in the UK', *British Journal of Psychiatry* 189, 109–17.

Sonnentag, S. and Bayer, U.-V. (2005) 'Switching off mentally: Predictors and consequences of psychological detachment from work during off-job time', *Journal of Occupational Health Psychology* 10, 393–414.

Spinella, M., Yang, B. and Lester, D. (2007) 'Prefrontal systems in financial processing', *Journal of Socio Economics* 36, 480–89.

Squires, S. (2007) 'Nonstop office: maybe it's good for you', *Washington Post*, 19 January 2007. Available at www.washingtonpost.com/wpdyn/content/article/2007/01/19/AR2007011901447.html. Accessed on 5 June 2011.

Steptoe, A., Wright, C., Kunz-Ebrecht, S.R. and Iliffe, S. (2006) 'Dispositional optimism and health behaviour in community-dwelling older people: Associations with healthy ageing', *British Journal of Health Psychology* 11 (1), 71–84.

Strazdins, L. (2002) 'Emotional work and emotional contagion', in N.M. Ashkanasy, W.J. Zerbe and C.E.J. Hartel (eds) *Managing Emotions in the Workplace*. New York: Sharpe, 232–50.

Sunday Times (2009) 'The Best Companies To Work For'. Available at http//business.timesonline.co.uk/tol/business/career_and_jobs/article6850595.ece, accessed on 26 February 2010.

Sy, T., Tram, S. and O'Hara, L. (2006) 'Relation of employee and manager to job satisfaction and performance', *Journal of Vocational Behaviour* 68 (3), 461–73.

Taylor, G.J., Parker, J.D.A. and Bagby, R.M. (1999) 'Emotional intelligence and the emotional brain: Points of convergence and implications for psychoanalysis', *Journal of the American Academy of Psychoanalysis* 27, 339–54.

Taylor, M.F., Brice, J., Buck, N. and Prentice-Lane, E. (2004) *British Household Panel Survey User Manual* vol. A: Introduction, Technical Report and Appendices. Colchester: University of Essex.

Taylor, M.P., Pevalin, D.J. and Todd, J. (2007) 'The psychological costs of unsustainable housing commitments', *Psychological Medicine* 37, 1027–36.

Terkel, S. (1972) *Working*. New York: Avon Books.

London Times (2011) 'Every one in five: young and jobless', 13 April.

London Times (2009) 'White and blue-eyed to blame for global crisis', 27 March.

Tindle, H.A., Chang, Y-F., Kuller, L.H., Manson, J.E., Robinson, J.G., Rosal, M.C., Siegle, G.J. and Matthews, K.A. (2009) 'Optimism, cynical hostility, and incident coronary heart disease and mortality in the Women's Health Initiative'. Circulation. 120, 656–662.

Towers Perrin-ISR (2006) The ISR *Employee Engagement Report*.

Turnley, W.H. and Feldman, D.C. (2000) 'Re-examining the effects of psychological contract violations: Unmet expectations and job dissatisfaction as mediators', *Journal of Organizational Behaviour* 21, 1–25.

Tyers, C. and Lucy, D. (2008) Available at http://www.hse.gov.uk/workplacehealth/jan08.pdf Workplace Health Connect, January 2008 progress report.

Ursano, R.J., Epstein, R.S. and Lazar, S.G. (2002) 'Behavioral responses to illness: Personality and personality disorders', in M.G. Wise and J.R. Rundell (eds) *The American Psychiatric Publishing Textbook of Consultation-Liaison Psychiatry. Psychiatry in the Medically Ill*, 2nd edn. Washington D.C.: American Psychiatric Publishing, 107–25.

US Dept of Health and Human Services (1996) Available at http://www.nhlbi.nih.gov/health/public/heart/obesity/phy_act.htm.

USA Today (2008) 'If the US economy were a car, all of its warning lights must be flashing red', 19 March.

Vahtera, J., Kivimaki, M., Pentti, J., Linna, A., Virtanen, M., Virtanen, P. and Ferrie, J.E. (2004) 'Organisational downsizing, sickness absence and mortality: 10-town prospective cohort study', *British Medical Journal*, 328(7439), 555.

Van der Klink, J.J.L., Blonk, R.W.B., Schene, A.H. and van Dijk, F.J.H. (2001) 'The benefits of interventions for work-related stress', *American Journal of Public Health* 92, 270–76.

Villanueva, D. and Djurkovic, N. (2009) 'Occupational stress and intention to leave among employees in small and medium enterprises', *International Journal of Stress Management* 16 (2), 124–37.

Voit, S. (2001) 'Work-site health and fitness programs: Impact on the employee and employer', *Work* 16, 273–86.

Wall, T.D., Bolden, R.I., Borrill, C.S., Golya, D.A., Hardy, G.E., Haynes, G., Rick, J.W., Shapiro, D.A. and West, M.A. (1997) 'Minor psychiatric disorder in NHS Trust staff: Occupational and gender differences', *British Journal of Psychiatry* 171, 519–23.

Warr, P.B. (2007) *Work, Happiness and Unhappiness.* Mahwah, NJ: Erlbaum.

Warr, P.B. (1999) 'Well-being in the workplace', in D. Kahneman, E. Diener and N. Schwartz (eds) *Well-being: The Foundations of Hedonic Psychology.* New York: Russell Sage.

Warr, P.B. (1987) *Psychology at Work*, 3rd edn. London: Penguin.

Watson, D., Clark, L.A. and Tellegen, A. (1988) 'Development and validation of brief measures of positive and negative affect: The PANAS Scales', *Journal of Personality and Social Psychology* 54, 1063–70.

Watson, D. and Pennebaker, J.W. (1989) 'Health complaints, stress and distress: Exploring the central role of negative affectivity', *Psychological Review* 96, 234–54.

Weinberg, A. (2008) *Management Coaching Initiative Final Report.* University of Salford, Salford, UK.

Weinberg, A. and Cooper, C.L. (2007) *Surviving the Workplace: A Guide to Emotional Well-being at Work.* London: Thomson Learning.

Weinberg, A. and Cooper, C.L. (2003) 'Stress among national politicians elected to Parliament for the first time', *Stress and Health* 19, 111–17.

Weinberg, A. and Creed, F. (2000) 'Stress and psychiatric disorder in healthcare professionals and hospital staff', *The Lancet* 355, 533–37.

Weinberg, A., Sutherland, V.J. and Cooper, C.L. (2010) *Organizational Stress Management: A Strategic Approach.* Basingstoke: Palgrave Macmillan.

Williams, P.G., Smith, T., Gunn, H.E. and Uchino, B.N. (2011) 'Personality and stress: Individual differences in exposure, reactivity, recovery and restoration', in R.J. Contrada and A. Baum (eds) *Handbook of Stress Science: Biology, Psychology, and Health.* New York: Springer, 231–45.

Williams, S., Dale, J., Glucksman, E. and Wellesley, A. (1997) 'Senior house officers' work related stressors, psychological distress, and confidence in performing clinical tasks in accident emergency: A questionnaire study', *British Medical Journal* 314, 713–18.

Winefield, A.H., Gillespie, N., Stough, C., Dua, J., Hapuarachchi, J. and Boyd, C. (2003) 'Occupational stress in Australian university staff', *International Journal of Stress Management* 10, 51–63.

Worrall, L. and Cooper, C.L. (2001) 'The long working hours culture', *European Business Forum* 6, 48–53.

Yu, S., Yarnell, J.W.G., Sweetnam, P.M. and Murray, L. (2003) 'What level of physical activity protects against premature cardiovascular death? The Caerphilly study', *Heart* 89, 502–06.

Zheng, H., Ehrlich, F. and Amin, J. (2009) 'Economic evaluation of the direct healthcare cost savings resulting from the use of walking interventions to prevent coronary heart disease in Australia', *International Journal of Health Care Finance and Economics* 10(2), 187–201. DOI: 10.1007/s10754-009-9074-2

Zimmern, A. (nd) *Marcus Aurelius – Meditations*. London: Walter Scott.